GW00632311

AS THE TWIG IS BENT

AS THE TWIG IS BENT

The Childhood Recollections of Sixteen Prominent Australians

Presented by Terry Lane

DOVE COMMUNICATIONS
MELBOURNE

Published by Dove Communications Pty Ltd
60-64 Railway Road, Blackburn, Victoria, 3130
Australia

Designed by Brian Seddon

Second Printing March 1980
Third Printing July 1981
Fourth Printing October 1982
Fifth Printing October 1984

© Copyright 1979 Terry Lane
All rights reserved.
No part of this book may be reproduced without
permission in writing from the publishers.

National Library of Australia
Cataloguing in Publication data
As the Twig is Bent
ISBN 0 85924 133 5
ISBN 0 85924 132 7 Paperback
1 Australia — Biography
I Lane, Terry, 1939—, ed.
920'.094

Typeset by Dove Communications
Printed in Australia by Brownhall Printing

'Tis education forms the common mind:
Just as the twig is bent the tree's inclined.

Alexander Pope

TO MY MOTHER AND FATHER
who chose me from those available
and made me their own

Acknowledgements

'Intolerance', a poem by Kath Walker, from *We are Going*, Jacaranda, 1964, p. 37.

Extract from *The Helpman Family Story*, by Mary Helpman, Rigby, 1967, p. 48.

Extract from *The Unspeakable Adams*, by Phillip Adams, Thomas Nelson (Aust.) Ltd, 1977, p.

All photos by Terry Lane except Manning Clark and

Charles Mackerras (*The Herald*) and Bob Ansett.

Contents

Introduction

The great anxiety common to almost all conscientious parents is this: 'What am I doing to my children? Here I am, undertaking the most important task entrusted to human beings, the nurturing and forming of other human beings, and I am doing it without training or guidance. Will my children, when they reach adulthood, regard me with contempt and hatred for messing up their lives psychically, physically and intellectually when they were at their most impressionable and vulnerable?'

Fashions in childrearing come and go, covering the entire spectrum from *laissez faire* to extreme disciplinarianism. There are parents who believe that their children should be left to discover their own moral values, intellectual interests and vocations. There are others who consider that a parent has the responsibility to play a more positive role in shaping the child's life. There are professional advocates of both extremes.

Parents ponder the heredity versus environment puzzle, wondering which is the more influential in the development of the child. Some are anxious to make their child's path smoother than their own, while others fear that they may simply be trying to fulfil their own frustrated ambitions through their offspring.

What follows in this book is an attempt to discover what, if anything, sixteen prominent, accomplished and creative Australians had in common in their childhood experiences. Is there some vital ingredient in their relationships with their parents or in their education or discipline which they all share and which has predisposed them to success? Can the anxious parent find in the lives of the leaders of their society some guidance for their own role as spiritual, intellectual and physical guardians of their progeny?

Each chapter of this book is the transcript of a recorded interview with the subject. The only alterations to their words have been made to eliminate the interviewer's questions and provide a form of literary continuity.

There are few people who can be completely honest and open about their childhood experiences. Most people have certain painful memories. To disclose these would be to reveal character weaknesses we would rather leave hidden. Professor Manning Clark gives an example of this reticence when he talks of 'a shadow' falling across his path. This is a tantalising reference to an incident that we intuitively feel must be relevant to understanding the man, but he is prepared to go so far and no further.

In gathering the material the interpretation placed by the individuals on the childhood experiences was never challenged. Sometimes it may be necessary to read between the lines to discover what a person is really saying about his or her life as a child. On the other hand some of those interviewed have obviously reflected at such length on their childhood experiences that there is always the danger of their self-assessment being over-sophisticated, with significance being attached to childhood experiences and events which are in themselves too trivial to bear the weight of interpretation placed on them.

The sixteen people in this book gave their time generously for the interviews and without conditions in almost all cases. In spite of the warning just given it must be said that they were almost all very frank and ready to share some of the pain as well as the joy of their childhood years. I am profoundly grateful to them all for giving both their time and a small part of themselves to this project.

To my wife Valda, typist and speller *extraordinaire*, and a constant source of encouragement, I wish to express my deep gratitude.

Robert Helpmann

Robert Helpmann was born on Good Friday, 9 April, 1909, the son of Mary and Sam (James Murray) Helpman. (Sir Robert added the second n to his name when he was in his early twenties because it had a more foreign and theatrical appearance.) In 1932 he left for London to dance with a newly-formed ballet company at Sadler's Wells, assuming the star role of Satan in the ballet Job when the Russian star was unavailable. By the end of 1933 Helpmann was a success. From that beginning he went on to make a reputation as a dancer, accompanying Dame Margot Fonteyn in many ballets. He also developed his talents as a choreographer and producer. Later he added acting to his accomplishments and eventually returned to Australia in 1955, after an absence of twenty-three years, to tour with the Old Vic in a season of Shakespeare's plays, playing in The Merchant of Venice, The Taming of The Shrew and Measure for Measure. His co-star was Katharine Hepburn.

Helpmann was awarded the C.B.E. in 1964, named Australian of the Year in 1966 and knighted in 1968. From 1965 to 1976 he was Director of the Australian Ballet and has been Artistic Director of the Adelaide Festival since 1970.

Sir Robert has produced and directed plays and operas as well as ballet. He has appeared in numerous films, including the Australian productions The Mango Tree and Patrick. One of his later stage productions was Dracula, starring John Waters.

In 1976, a few weeks before the premiere of the Australian Ballet's most ambitious project under Helpmann, the three-act ballet of The Merry Widow, his contract as Director of the Australian Ballet was not renewed. Since then Helpmann has continued to work in Australia as an actor and producer and also as entrepreneur.

There is no doubt that Sir Robert Helpmann has made an invaluable contribution to the arts in Australia, both personally and by bringing to Australia his friends Margot Fonteyn, Rudolf Nureyev and Katharine Hepburn.

1

I never lost my devotion to the theatre, and when in the second year of our marriage I knew I was going to have a child my secret hope was that he or she, as the case might be, would do in the theatrical world what I had been prevented from doing.

Mary Helpman

My mother was a most remarkable woman. She knew what she wanted and nothing was going to stop her. I think I've inherited a little bit of that from her. She was also very funny—a marvellous mimic. She had very strong likes and dislikes. She was completely responsible for my ever becoming anything that I am—if I am anything. It was absolutely and entirely due to my mother.

She loved the theatre herself and when she was at boarding school (her father was on a sheep station in South Australia) she read that a company was giving auditions for a play by Barrie. Now my mother's mother was Scottish, so my mother was very good at doing a Scottish accent and she auditioned for, and got, the part of a little Scottish maid. She was thrilled. But her mother heard of it and flew into a rage, went to the school and dragged her home. She was never allowed to go on the stage until later, as a teenager, she became an amateur actress, playing in all the Shakespeare plays. She knew them very well and when my father fell in love with her she forced him to play scenes with her, which I think must have been very much against his will.

Even before I could read, my mother taught me scenes from Shakespeare. I remember doing the balcony scene from *Romeo and Juliet*, and very soon, realising that Juliet had a better part than Romeo in the scene, I decided to be Juliet. I can remember distinctly standing up in my cot reciting to my mother as Romeo.

She used to dress up, and put on clothes for me and I remember that the thing I loved mostly was the red robe that she wore as Portia. Many years later, every time Katharine Hepburn appeared as Portia she suddenly turned into my mother. It was a most extraordinary feeling, as I played Shylock with Kate, to see this transformation—really very odd.

To succeed on the stage you need to have exhibitionist tendencies and my mother encouraged me in them. My father just gave up—he didn't understand at all. Ultimately he was responsible for my going on stage, but he left me alone, and I didn't care about what anybody, other than my mother and father, thought. I didn't care about the other children and I didn't suffer very much from it. Nobody crushed me down. I was encouraged by my mother and my original dance teacher, Nora Stewart, and practically everybody played along with me. I was rather forceful for a child!

I must say my mother never pressured me—she didn't have to. I did everything to fulfil my own ambition, so she never had to pressure me to go to dancing lessons or voice lessons. I was only too willing to go! I didn't realise until much later in life that my mother had this ambition for me. I thought the ambition was purely mine. I didn't realise that it was instilled instinctively from her and that I was fulfilling what my mother wanted me to.

My mother and I were terribly close. Although she adored my brother Max it never entered her head that he wanted to be an actor. Of course both my brother and sister are now very successful actors, but mother concentrated more on me. I was the first— the eldest—and therefore her attention was concentrated on me. Max and Sheila's ambitions were a little bit overshadowed by mine, which I've always thought was responsible for a feeling of tension between my brother and myself. He's a bit shy of me still, after all these years.

As I said before, my father, in a curious way, was responsible for my going on the stage. I was always trailing around the house dressed as something or other and had this ambition to dance, which he couldn't understand. But once, after he returned from a business trip to Melbourne, he told mother that he wanted to talk to me. He said: 'There's a girl in Melbourne who's got a company of dancers, and she seems good and she's agreed to take you as a student and you're going next week with your mother to Melbourne.' It never entered my head to ask who the girl was, and when I got to Melbourne it was Anna Pavlova. I'm afraid by the time it dawned on me to ask my father how he got into her dressing room and persuaded her to take me as a student both my father and Pavlova were dead, so I don't know to this day.

Father was a famous man in his line as an expert on cattle, sheep and wool. I think he naturally hoped that his eldest son would follow in his footsteps. When he finally settled for the fact that I wasn't going to I think that he hoped his second son would, which he did for a long time. He never consciously made me feel that he was resisting my theatrical ambitions. He may have discussed it with my mother, but he always came to see me dance. I remember I did a show called *Hello Hello* in which I was made up all over brown, and my father used to put on the body make-up for me, and then put me under the shower afterwards and wash it off. So if he opposed my ambitions I was never totally conscious of it, and I wouldn't have paid any attention anyway!

Among my childhood memories are recollections of the First World War which broke out when I was about five or six. I remember going to a hotel called the Grand Central and watching the first consignment of troops marching off down Rundle Street and my father holding me up to the window to see them going. Then we went down into the street and I can remember very clearly that I had a flag, a Union Jack or perhaps an Australian flag, and another child tore it off me and we had the most terrible fight. I also remember going around on the back of a wagon doing performances and collecting for the troops. I remember very clearly how my mother used to put up billy cans with presents in and send to the troops. I had a letter back from a soldier who had received our parcels and we started a long correspondence. I used to get these letters from him when I was about seven and then suddenly there was a pause—no letters came. He had been killed. I remember distinctly going out and waiting for the postman to come. Then all his things were sent to me because mine was the only name he had on him when he was found dead. He had a picture of me with my name on the back. He had no parents.

Other sad memories I have of childhood are the deaths of my grandmother and my mother's sister, Barbie. Aunt Barbie was a wonderful woman who also had a great influence on me. She was very artistic and sang beautifully. Both these deaths affected me enormously.

I was deeply upset when my grandmother died. It seemed I just couldn't believe it. I used to see her every day. I used to go and dance for her and she was my best audience. When we had moved from Mount Gambier my grandfather had bought three houses, one for my aunt, one for himself and his wife and one for my mother and father, very close together. So we were a closely-knit family. And the minute I got dressed up, if my mother was busy, I would rush to my grandmother, so when she died it was a terrible gap in my life.

But by and large I had a very, very happy childhood. In a way I suppose it was a sort of lonely childhood. I was six years older than Max and eight years older than Sheila and I lived in a sort of fantasy world. I used to go to the theatre every Saturday for the matinee, and we had a sewing woman, Miss Gilbert, who used to come in, and her first duty every Monday morning was to make the costume that I'd seen on the Saturday matinee. I would wear the costume when I got back from school each day. That would be my life until the following Saturday, and then I'd see a different play or movie and there'd be another costume. So I lived a sort of theatrical fantasy life.

I had a nursemaid once when I was very young (just out of the pram) who was very romantic. My father and mother were terribly worried because I was always sitting in the drawing room, covered in mosquito net with oleander flowers in my hair, and they thought I was going mad. However, as I said, the nursemaid, Violet, was very romantic and she used to find out where all the weddings in our suburb were so that she could go to watch the bride and groom come out. She would take me with her and the groom didn't appeal to me because he just had a suit on, but the bride always looked very theatrical and wonderful, so the minute I got home I dressed up as a bride. You know it's a curious thing, but when I met Frederick Ashton many years later and was telling him about this he said that he used to do the same thing in South America.

People who have achieved something outstanding in the theatre have many childhood experiences in common, you know. First, and obviously, there is the love of the theatre, even in childhood. Everybody I've asked, particularly people like Laurence Olivier and Alec Guinness, have never had any ambition other than the theatre—though oddly Kate, funnily enough, doesn't fit this pattern. She was a marvellous student. Very brilliant. She could have been anything you know—a great tennis player, a great golfer, a doctor or a lawyer.

We also have in common ambitious mothers. Freddy Ashton's mother was very ambitious for him in the theatre. He was the youngest of twelve brothers, and when his father died his mother brought him to England and put him to school there, and she was very anxious for him to go on the stage. They were very similar, Mrs Ashton and my mother—although I don't think Mrs Ashton was quite as forceful or quite as ambitious as my mother. My mother has written 'a leopard caring for her young has nothing on a ballet mother', and that's true. Ballet mothers are absolutely extraordinary. They're fiercer than leopards!

Another person who had a great influence on me was my first dancing teacher, Nora Stewart. She was a remarkable woman. One day I went to one of her ballet classes and I said, 'That's what I want to do!' She'd never had boys who wanted to do that before, so I did all the things with the girls, and danced on my points, which is why I've always had such very strong feet in the ballet. Nora influenced me enormously. She taught me what was good and what was bad as far as technique and dancing went. She used to give me all the dance magazines from America and from England.

Once, Nora Stewart's pupils gave a recital at the Exhibition Hall in Adelaide before Melba. I danced the Pizzicato from *Sylvia.* Because I did it better than any of the little girls I was dressed as a girl with a tutu, golden wig and everything. It was an enormous success and I had to do it again and at the end I took my wig off, much to everybody's amazement, including Melba's. She asked to meet me. I met her many times after that, but she always remembered me with, 'Oh, you're the little boy that I first saw as a little girl.'

My first role in the theatre was as a fairy in *The Merry Wives of Windsor*. All of Nora Stewart's little pupils went as fairies and that was my first time on stage. Then, of course, I graduated into doing solo dances in her break-ups. My first professional engagement was in a summer theatre in the Exhibition Gardens in Adelaide when J. C. Williamsons ran a thing called 'The So and So's' which was really the equivalent of an English concert party. I was engaged as a solo dancer there.

I think I inherited from my mother a drive for perfection. I suppose I had a built-in thing that could distinguish between good and bad performances. I can remember going to see a production of Shakespeare by a very famous actor, Allan Wilkie and his wife, Frediswyde Hunter-Watts. They used to tour Australia and they were marvellous. And I can remember, even though I couldn't have been more than eight or nine at the time, suddenly thinking, 'My goodness, those two are good, but the rest are terrible!' So I learned at a very early age to distinguish between the first-class and the second-class—and I think that's an innate ability. The minute I went with Pavlova I saw the difference between her and other dancers. There are others who may have a stronger technique but she, like Fonteyn and Maria Callas, like Nureyev, she had that something you can't explain that made her exquisitely perfect.

It's probably not surprising that I loathed school—or at least College. I went to Prince Alfred College in Adelaide and hated it. That was my fault. Many years later, when I went back to the school with Katharine Hepburn, I realised how nice the masters were. I must have been a terrible problem, but I just couldn't be bothered. I couldn't think why I had to work out x^2 equals so many, as it had nothing to do with me. All I wanted to do was to go to the theatre or the cinema and to dance or act; the boredom of class just killed me. I regret it deeply. I wish now that I had had a marvellous education and could do things like read Greek plays in the original language. But at the time I just couldn't be bothered.

Sometimes I think that if I'd been a child of the 1970s I would never have done what I have. Television turns children into passive consumers of entertainment. I had to make my own entertainment. I had to invent theatres. In the drawing room of our home in Adelaide there were swing doors which led into the passage, which had other doors going off it, so I used to force my family and my mother's friends to sit there while I entertained them. I don't see children doing that today because of television. They rush home from school and put on the television. I do myself, so if I'd had it as a child I don't know that my creative mind would ever have been exercised to the extent that it was.

Never, for one second, have I ever contemplated any vocation other than the theatre. I have no regrets at all about my childhood, apart perhaps, from wishing that my education had heightened my knowledge of literature. But education wouldn't have influenced me in any way to do anything else but be in the theatre. So I have no regrets, but I don't have any great sense of achievement, either. I don't know why this is. Before I went overseas I used to think: 'If only I could become the leading dancer in a ballet company, I'd be happy.' Well, I became the leading dancer, and I wasn't all that happy. Then I thought: 'Now, if only I could play Hamlet with a Shakespearean company . . . ' Well, I did—and my life's gone on like that, and I don't feel any sense of achievement. I think if I did I probably wouldn't do anything else. I've asked a lot of people about this. I've asked Kate: 'Do you consciously feel satisfaction?' I always find that when I'm working on a ballet or a play, the minute I start rehearsing that play or that ballet I immediately think of the next one. If I run out of ideas the sure-fire way for me to think of something is to start work on some project and I immediately start thinking of something else. I have to fight this in case it stops the concentration on what I'm doing now. So I'm conscious of having achieved things, but there's no great satisfaction. I'm always amazed when people say: 'Oh, well I feel so satisfied.' I never have felt that way.

Manning Clark

Charles Manning Hope Clark is the son of the late Rev. C. H. Clark, an Anglican clergyman. Now Emeritus Professor of Australian History at the Australian National University, Manning Clark is widely known through his books, including his major work A History of Australia. One of his recent books, In Search Of Henry Lawson, caused a good deal of argument about his particular view of that Australian writer.

Professor Clark won the Henry Lawson Arts Award in 1969; the Australian Literary Society Gold Medal in 1970 and the Age Book Prize in 1974. In 1975 he was made a Companion of the Order of Australia. In late 1978 and early 1979 he was Visiting Professor of Australian Studies at Harvard University.

Manning Clark has become an outspoken critic of Australian society in his books, articles, speeches and broadcasts, expressing a profound pessimism about the future. The events of November 1975, 'that year in which the money-changers and accountants—the men with a passion for interest rates seemingly as dionysiacal as the passion of some men for "other things"—were to have their terrible day of triumph', have left him deeply disturbed. Because of his defence of the Whitlam Government and his criticism of the 'men with hearts of walnuts' who engineered Whitlam's downfall there was a storm over his commission to broadcast the Boyer Lectures on the ABC in 1976. An attempt to censor the lectures before they were recorded was thwarted when it was made public.

Professor Clark has been described as a 'twentieth-century Jeremiah' prophesying doom for our society as it is today, which he calls an 'over-ripe . . . age of ruins . . .'. And he adds that '. . . to judge by that other example of an over-ripe age, such an age generally precedes a dark and barbarous age.'

11

I was born on the 3 March 1915 in Burwood, Sydney.

My earliest memories are of my father coming back from the war in 1919. I was sitting on the lawn in the back garden of the house in Park Street when I saw him walking towards me. He seemed very pleased to see me and I, sixty years later, can only hope that my response was as warm and generous as his welcome to me. About the same time (I am not sure now of the date) I can remember seeing the plane in which Keith and Ross Smith had flown from London to Sydney. I remember it flying over our house. My mother said in later years that I surprised them all by talking about the significance of their achievement, but as she was always inclined to hyperbole when talking about the gifts of her second son, I wonder now whether any such remark was ever made. I still, however, can see in my mind's eye that huge mechanical bird in the sky.

My father was born near Plumstead, London, in August 1878. He was the son of Thomas Clark, a carpenter who used to work in the Woolwich Arsenal. With the decline in employment in the arsenal during a depression at the end of the 1870s he decided to migrate to Australia. His wife came from an Irish family. They migrated to Sydney in 1881 and settled in St Peters. My father won a scholarship to St Andrew's Cathedral Choir School in Sydney, and later another scholarship to Moore Theological College. I remember him as a man who had gifts as a speaker, a man who believed passionately in loving kindness, a man who loved sport. When we were young he was always showing us how to play a late cut or a leg glance. Perhaps it was significant that at the end of each stroke he made a most elegant flourish with his bat. He was a clergyman but I do not know what his religious opinions were, or how deep was his faith in God and the life of the world to come. He loved music, especially Stainer's *Crucifixion* and Handel's *Messiah*. He used to love literature, especially Charles Dickens' *A Christmas Carol* and Nathaniel Hawthorne's *The*

Scarlet Letter. But by the time he reached fifty, or maybe even earlier, the great enthusiasms of his life seemed to fade and he was left with his passionate love of his children, his fishing and his stories about the past. I should add that he was a brilliant raconteur and had a keen eye for and a great love of eccentrics. He told wonderful stories of the years when he was chaplain of Long Bay Gaol in Sydney. The warm-hearted, generous Charles Henry William Clark would have forgiven everyone, but with the other side of his nature he believed the world was inhabited by Alexander the Coppersmiths, men who had done him and all people of his temperament great evil. I doubt whether he ever learned to keep out of the way of those spiritual bullies who bothered him. He liked to believe even they would respond to kindness, but was always being terribly hurt by them. I sometimes think that was why he was so fond of fishing and playing the piano; a man with rod or music was safe from his tormentors. I should add that he loved watching cricket (he always barracked for England, the country of his birth) and football (he barracked for Geelong because his wife's family had been pioneers in that district). He was greatly liked by people. When he died in January 1951 the church was filled, partly with all those misfits, the people who could not manage life at all—the creatures whom his God seemed to have forgotten.

My mother came from a quite different social class. She was the great-great-granddaughter of the Reverend Samuel Marsden and was born in Dunedin, New Zealand, in 1877. Her family on her father's side belonged to the country gentry of New South Wales and Victoria. She went to the Presbyterian Ladies' College in Croydon, Sydney, where she won the prize in her matriculation year for history and English and chose T. B. Macaulay's *History of England.* It is now one of my proudest possessions. She also played the piano very well. Indeed she was proficient in all the skills taught to women at the end of the nineteenth century.

Judging by family photographs she must have been very beautiful when she met my father, who was then a curate at St John's Church of England in Ashfield, Sydney. For a number of years they wrote most moving letters to each other about their hopes of playing a part in presenting the image of Christ to the people of Sydney.

By nature and training my mother was a woman who seemed to believe that God's Elect were those who could observe the rather harsh laws prescribed by her God to those who hoped to enter the Kingdom of Heaven. She had an unbounded charity and power of forgiveness to those who either could not or would not observe such laws. She had inherited from her family all the prejudices of her class about the 'lower orders', but superimposed on these she held to the teachings of Christ about her duty to 'the least of the little ones'. She had a deep and unshakeable faith in God. In all the great crises of her life she asked for Divine help. When my sister was dying of infantile paralysis, I remember that all the members of the family save my mother wept and were quite overwhelmed with a sense of an unbearable loss. My mother, looking most majestic, her face like that of a person transfigured, said she would pray. And so she did at my sister's bedside. My sister came through that ordeal, because she had a great strength to endure, but once the crisis was over my mother began to fade in strength and to lose interest in the world. Like my father she had a great capacity for love, a love she gave most generously to all her three children. She had an eye for what was in other people, for what came up from inside them. She was a great believer in the injunction, 'Judge not'.

In the last ten or so years of her life her interests did not extend beyond a passionate concern for and a never-ending anxiety about the welfare of her children. Like most human beings she was a bundle of contradictions. When I was a child, she warned me against ever being friendly with Germans: 'They're very clever,

Man dear.' She warned me that many human beings were 'so peculiar' that she must ask me to promise never to speak to them. Yet a minute later she might speak as though all God's children were of equal significance. In many ways she was a formidable mother with great power in persuading us all to accept her view of the world. When we were being silly she used to warn us not to behave in that way because other people might think we were what she called 'mental', or she would ask us to desist from any behaviour which offended her on the bizarre grounds that we were making her feel 'dizzy'. When I told her of some of my strange ideas in childhood, she always let me know when they were outrageous in her eyes by saying: 'Go and ask the others, Man dear, and see what they think.' Her great misfortune was that she made little if any use of her considerable intellectual and artistic gifts after she was fifty. Men and women in all walks of life revered her. I suspect now that few ever came close to her, not because she was off-putting or stand-offish, but because she obviously measured people by standards they were unlikely to reach. She loved giving things to those in need. She had some of the air of a very special person and great stores of popular wisdom. 'Envy is a very terrible thing, Man dear,' she would say. When a shadow fell across my path in 1929 she did everything to help, but to my puzzlement she told me she wondered what she had done for God to punish her in this sort of way. She retained to the end her simple belief that God (she always called Him 'Our Father') would be more helpful to the afflicted than any doctors or scientists. When she began to decline in health and intellectual power I had ceased to be a child but could not bridge the gulf she had built between herself and the outside world. Perhaps she was one of the very few genuine believers I have ever known. Looking back to childhood days, I remember that the very few real believers who came to the various vicarages in which we lived were always deeply drawn to her. They always seemed to recognise each other at once and then a light would come into my mother's eye. I think of her even now, across the wild years, as someone who belonged to 'the Kingdom of all believers'.

I do not know which of my parents I most resemble. My interest in conveying a vision of human life by telling a story probably came from my father. I would like to think that my single-mindedness and determination to keep going, to endure to the end, came from my mother. So far that precious gift of faith, which sustained her through all her great spiritual pain ('There are things in my life, Man dear, I hope you will never know anything about'), has not been given to me, though she probably planted in me the 'thirst to believe'. Who knows?

I wouldn't call myself a believer in any particular religious creed, but I think it would be fair to say that many times in my life I've wanted to believe but there were all sorts of reasons why I could not share my mother's faith. What influenced me in childhood was the perception of a great gap between what people professed to believe and how they behaved, and from that I began to doubt whether they really did believe. I wasn't at all influenced by any talk of a conflict between science and religion.

But I do believe in a mystery at the heart of things—that one has a sense of something outside the world of the senses in the presence of such things as nature, the ocean, love, music. I think these are intimations that there is something beyond the world of what you see and touch and smell and so on—but, unlike my mother, I wouldn't give a name to it.

My parents had one great influence on me: they made me feel that the only persons who would rejoice when something deeply pleasing happened were my mother and my father. They were the great source of inspiration, they were the ones who had neverending faith in their prodigal son. I believe we are all children until our parents die. Then we are deprived of the only people in the world who know what we are talking about.

We moved about a great deal when I was a child. We lived first in Burwood, Sydney; then in Kempsey, in New South Wales in 1920 or 1921; then in Cowes on Phillip Island, Victoria, from about 1922 to 1924; then in Belgrave, Victoria, from 1924 to 1933, when childhood was over.

I have hazy memories of Burwood. One of them is of two of my mother's sisters trying to teach me to walk properly. (My father used to say I would fall over on a billiard table.) The other is of being stung by a bee when trying to bury my face in a white lily. I remember Kempsey mainly because we three children were afraid of a rooster which used to perch on our shoulders and peck at our faces. I remember also an old man who told me he was going to live forever by bathing his face in soot and kerosene and eating cabbage. I remember Cowes most vividly of all: the headmaster, Eric Hatfield, who was such a marvellous teacher, and the friendships with boys like Noel Cleland, Ronnie Bennell, Frank Towns, Colin Twyrold and a boy called Kent. When the time came to leave I was heart-broken, and much of life since has been a vain search to recapture the innocence of the days when we hunted rabbits or fished from the rocks or rode in the jinker or watched the sea or lay in bed at night in the vicarage listening to the wind in the pines, visited by doubts about what I had heard in the church and knowing for the first time that chill on contemplating the possibility of some future 'kingdom of nothingness'. I remember being tormented by doubts about whether what we learned in church could be true. As it was not fashionable to talk about such things I learned very early in life to 'hold my tongue' as the Psalmist puts it, and to wait for those rare moments when you met someone else who knew about that particular agony.

The life on Phillip Island became my Swannee River. Our family life was in harmony with all the wonders in the world about us. So I thought of our move to Belgrave as exile, and there I often spent the time between going to bed and falling asleep composing in my head doggerel verses about that other 'happy land far, far away'.

Life in the vicarage at both Cowes and Belgrave was always very lively. There seemed to be some church function or other every night from Sunday to Friday. At Belgrave I found this rather displeasing and began to sell newspapers in the main street at the weekend and sweets and lollies in the local picture theatre on Saturday night. Life in the vicarage impressed on my mind a quaint division of humanity between professed believers and unbelievers. It was my mother who created a strong religious atmosphere in the home. Out in the streets and in the picture theatre (the old 'Memorial Hall') I found a quite different life which beckoned to me and held out the promise of a different sort of happiness.

I do not remember ever hearing my father talk about politics, except when he told me how disenchanted he had been as a young man when two men in the Political Labour League in his suburb in Sydney 'imshied' to San Francisco, as my father put it, with all the assets of that branch. I suspect now that his sympathies were with Labor but that it was indiscreet and unwise for a man dependent on what his congregation put into the 'plate' each Sunday to declare his political beliefs. My mother always voted for the conservatives, cherishing all her life the delusion that they, like her father's family, were all 'gentlemen'.

My political education was begun at Belgrave by a man named Carter, part-owner of a garage in the main street. He told me about the Russian Revolution of 1917 and that it was the beginning of a new era in the history of mankind. I was tremendously excited by what he had to say, holding out as he did the promise that humanity would not always be weighed down by the tyranny of opinion which seemed to prevail in Belgrave.

I was greatly influenced by R.P. Franklin, the headmaster of Melbourne Grammar School, an Englishman who planted in my mind not only the idea of being an historian, but also his own faith that one day I would master all that was required for such a vocation. I also learned a little about the world of art, about the Greek view of the world from our neighbour at Belgrave, Dr Olaf Jörgensen, who told me about a world and a way of life quite different from the one sketched in the vicarage. I also continued to mix a lot with simple people—I remember in particular our maid Marge Thomson, Lettie Hale and Bella Green who all used to talk in our kitchen. I felt much more at home with them than at the more formal vicarage tea parties.

I have an older brother and a younger sister, both still alive. We are still very close although life drew each of us into a world to which the others were strangers.

I liked school at Cowes until Mr Hatfield left. I liked school at Belgrave because we had an excellent teacher, Mr Bleakley. I was less keen on Mont Albert Central School because like the other timid boys and girls I lived in fear of one of the masters. They were generous in their comments when I won a scholarship to Melbourne Grammar School. At first this last-named school was a very painful experience, especially in 1929, the year in which the shadow fell, but the later years were great years of discovery.

There are many contenders for my happiest childhood memory: a day at Pyramid Rock fishing with my father; seeing Lloyd Hagger take a mark on the Melbourne Cricket Ground; watching Harold Larwood bowl or Percy Chapman fielding in the covers; or hearing a piece of music; or succeeding in building a wireless which would work or seeing a rare look of pleasure steal over my mother's face when briefly she seemed to like what was happening; or talking to an adult about what life was all about while the sea heaved and hurled itself against the rocks at the Nobbies; or watching Kitty O'Donohue dance in the Memorial Hall at Belgrave.

The saddest memory is undoubtedly of the day my father and I finally left Phillip Island.

I remember the number of people who were drowned at Phillip Island. ('I want you to promise me, Man dear, you won't look at the body of a dead man. You won't be able to stand it.') Well, of course I did look, and am still haunted at times by that memory. I remember being made more and more aware of the difference in class between my father and my mother's family. I remember the 1920s as an apparently carefree everything-is-allowable time, and the occasional remarks by people like Mr Carter to the effect that our society would be destroyed one day.

I have six children of my own, five sons and one daughter, and I have consciously tried to shield them from one of the great wounds of my childhood: belonging to the genteel poor.

I have come to believe there is a chemistry of the body which explains many of the things that happen to a person in life, especially to those with a temperament which makes their life into what Thomas Hardy aptly called a 'tremulous stay'; which explains, too, the immediate bond one feels for those who have the same temperament, those strange affinities with kindred spirits which, like music and the sea and mountains, make life bearable. Such a temperament exposes a person to the temptation to pursue false idols. They are the ones to whom one risks what I call 'showing the view'. I have been lucky during the last twenty years to get to know many people with whom I have that bond of tenderness and sympathy.

My mother's talk about the past of her family roused my interest in the history of our country. She used to talk a lot about all the people in the very early period who, like herself, had some family connection with the Marsdens, the Hassalls or the Hopes. My father was fairly silent about his past, except for some lively stories about fishing in Cook's River with a bent pin and string, and being able to take a girl out in his Sydney for a shilling from which he would have twopence left to buy 'a bucket of prawns'. At the age of five I was told by my great-grandmother, Catharine Hope (*nee* Hassall and granddaughter of Samuel Marsden), she being then ninety-seven or ninety-eight, about a man called the Reverend Samuel Marsden who was said to be a cruel man. She wanted me to know that Marsden was not cruel: he was severe. I had no idea what she was talking about but can still see her as a being not of this world. As a child she had known John Macarthur and James Macarthur. Perhaps her words started up something inside me. But it was not until I learned about my father's family and had linked them with the boys with whom I had felt at ease at Cowes (boys like Plugger Bennell, as he was known: remembering how they always called me Mannin') that I saw the order in the chaos and that my work must be about the people of Australia whom I had loved. I saw that I must not be disquieted anymore by those spiritual bullies who had sometimes made my life a hell. I saw that having the love and the faith of such people brought all things together, even slaking some of that never-ending thirst to believe.

Perhaps my childhood was always at the elbow, as it were, helping me to dream the dream that one day I might put down on paper the story of why we are as we are and why, wherever I am, whether in Moscow, London, New York or at Harvard, I know deep down where I belong and that Australia is always for me the 'shire for men who understand'.

But it is also a place where many people seem to belong to a different world from mine. Some of them are provoked to great wrath by what I try to say. That too has been part of what Henry James called my 'complex fate'. There is one side of me which believes all those shouters and mockers will gradually fade away, but another part tells me they are with me forever in Australia— that Australia belongs to them.

Kath Walker

Kath Walker M.B.E. is one of Australia's most successful poets if success is measured in the number of copies of her books which have been sold. When her first book of poems, We Are Going, *was published in 1964, it went into seven editions in seven months. She was not only the first Aborigine to have poetry published, but was the first Australian poet to have a collection of poetry published in America. Next to C.J. Dennis she is the bestselling Australian poet of all time. Her poems help whites to see the world from the black point of view in a way which prose could hardly accomplish.*

Kath Walker was born on Stradbroke Island near Brisbane, and at thirteen started work as a domestic. She later tried to become a nurse, but was rejected because she was an Aborigine. She has been Queensland state secretary of the Federal Council of the Aboriginal Advancement League and secretary of the Queensland State Council for the Advancement of Aborigines and Torres Strait Islanders.

In 1966 she published her second book of poems, The Dawn is at Hand. *Since then she has written a book for children,* Stradbroke Childhood *and the enlightenment of children is now her principal interest. She travels around Australia with a film biography,* Shadow Sister, *which has been seen by many thousands of children. On Stradbroke Island, where she is again living, she opens her home, Moongalba, to hundreds of visiting children every year.*

Kath Walker was born Kathleen Jean Mary Ruska in 1920.

When the white glug contemptuously
Says 'nigger', it is plain to me
He is of lower grade than we.

When we hear from the white elite
'We won't have abos in our street,'
Their Christianity's a cheat.

Dark children coming home in tears,
Hurt and bewildered by their jeers—
I think Christ weeps with you, my dears.

People who say, by bias driven,
That colour must not be forgiven,
Would snub the Carpenter in heaven.

Kath Walker

In that poem I'm writing from my own experience as a child, because, like all Aboriginal children I experienced that sort of intolerance. You're the best of friends with the white kids until you're
having a difference of opinion with them and then they bring up
your colour. I remember once getting so angry with a boy of the
same age as me, when he said: 'You blasted blacks! You think you
own the country.' Quite forgetting that once upon a time my
people did. He told me that he was going to get me and flog me
into the ground, and I remember, very dramatically, carrying a
stockwhip on the horse when I went in to get the meat at six
o'clock in the morning.

I was brought up in a mixture of black and white children, and
from the time I was born, from the time I could make sense of
myself, I realised that as far as whites were concerned I was supposed to occupy an inferior place in society. We've never been
without that feeling. But there was certainly never a time when I
wished I was white. Good God, no! I was always ashamed of what
the white people did. I didn't want to be white and I still don't

24

want to be white. I'd hate to be white, which is the racist coming out in me now, because I couldn't have on my conscience what the whites have to live with and I'm glad I'm black for that reason. You'd have to be a damned strong, unfeeling person to be a white person.

As a child I felt that in the white-dominated society we were the tailenders in everything. We weren't allowed to go to dances. The dance floors were for whites only. Blacks were not admitted. When we went swimming at our own lake there was a place put aside for whites and we had to go right away so that we wouldn't look upon the bodies of the white people while we were swimming. There had to be a lot of distance between us, and we were the second-class citizens. I didn't *feel* I was a second-class citizen, but I was put into that position.

Sometimes I think, even worse than the utter racism of it all, were the do-gooders. Women would come out and smother us with twisted-up thoughts, which they called 'love': 'Yes, we'll look after you, darling. I know you can't do it yourself so I'll do it for you.' They're still around bedevilling us. They are whites who can't have known society and peace and harmony and can't live with themselves. They feel important by living and collaborating with what they consider a lower class of people. When I was a child they were all around.

I spent my childhood on Stradbroke Island, a few kilometres off the coast from Brisbane. Near one end of the island there was an old people's home called 'The Dunwich Benevolent Asylum for the Aged and Infirm'—and it was a socialist government that gave it that title, I might add. There was a white staff at the home and I went to school with their children.

My father was ganger of an Aboriginal work gang. The Aboriginals had to do all the dirty work: they were wharfies, road-makers and drain cleaners. My father was a very straight and determined man, and although he left school at the age of ten to work as a shepherd boy, he was a very learned man. He didn't just leave his learning in the Aboriginal field, but he learned in the white field as well. He was a man who could turn his hand to any darn thing, be it fixing a motor or whatever. He was a very logical man and he bought us toys like iron hoops which he had made by the blacksmith. He taught us how to make shanghais and how to flatten out galvanised iron and sharpen all the edges, making a sharpened square of iron which is marvellous for getting a mullet through the water—*choom!* And he built us tools for the logical reason that we had to bring the food home, so most of our play things were tools.

From my father I learnt about nature and the sea. He loved the sea and I learnt from him how to respect it and not to muck up this old Quandamooka, which is what we called Moreton Bay. Quandamooka is a very beautiful woman but she can also be a very ugly one, and I learnt from my father when to leave her and when to go back to her and how to live in balance with nature. You only took enough food to feed yourself.

I was second-last in a family of seven children and my father, who worked for the government, got three pounds a week plus rations to feed the kids. We'd have died on the rations if we didn't know how to live Aboriginal-style. We belonged to the Noonuckle tribe of Stradbroke Island and although we were receiving a white education we were still receiving the education of Aboriginals on how to survive. We threw all the white man's tucker away. The tapioca—what muck!—we fed to the chooks, and we lived on parrots and bandicoots and dugong and fish and mud oysters, which we call 'quampee'. Dugong tastes smashing. We only took three a year, which was our limit. When you cook dugong it looks like a piece of corner-cut topside, but it's much nicer than that. Our delicacy from the dugong was the bacon which one of the old men used to cure for us. And grumpii sausage, made from the intestine of the dugong, was another favourite. Each family, according to its size, got a piece of the intestine and when the tide was in, my mother used to get us to take it out into the water and play tug-of-war with it. We didn't know it then, but of course we were cleaning it out in the salt water. Then she would boil it, and while the intestine was boiling she would mix the heart, liver and flesh and put herbs from the garden into it and use that to stuff the sausage. She would tie it at the end and boil it again. The Scots call it 'haggis'! It's very, very rich and very beautiful.

Bandicoot tastes like chicken. We all had bandicoot traps. You can't really knock the balance of bandicoots because they breed every month—seven kids a month! They're still on the island in droves, because we no longer eat them. We believed that if we ate them while we had a full belly we'd be punished. That's why we leave the dugong alone now because we feel if we took it now, when we have plenty of white man's food, the good spirit would punish us by taking one of the tribe.

My father was a stubborn man and I think I have inherited that from him. He didn't do much of the rousing around home, mum did most of that and whenever mum complained about me roaming around all over the place he used to tell her to leave me alone. 'She's different' he'd say. I remember the first night he said that. They'd had an argument and I wasn't supposed to be listening. In the end he got really mad and said: 'Leave her alone, she's different.' Mum was complaining because he wouldn't take a hand in chastising me. I was always roaming everywhere and she could never find me. Well, the last thing I wanted to be was different and I really cried myself to sleep that night because I thought my father had deserted me because I didn't know what he meant by 'different'. But he was paying me a compliment I suppose.

When I asked him questions he would say, 'Oh, girl—you're always reaching for the moon. One day you'll get it and it'll turn to cheese in your hand.' That's what he used to say when I'd get him exasperated and he didn't want to answer any more questions.

I was conscious of being a sticky beak. I wanted to know all sorts of things. I remember once bringing in a little golden pig-fish which I had found floating upside down near home. I took a bucket and brought it in and asked if I could keep it. Dad said that it wouldn't live and I asked why not. He told me that it was not made to live on land and that anyway, it was dying. (It had been hurt in the fishermen's nets.) I said: 'He won't die—I'll keep him awake.' And I tried hard to keep it alive, but the next day it was dead. I didn't like my father very much for being right and me being wrong, but it was my first lesson in seeing life and death as it was. That's the way I liked it to be—he never hid anything like that from us. That's life—and that's death.

My brother died at nineteen when I was only nine and I remember listening to the old people talking. One man asked: 'Will he be buried here?' And my imagination ran away. I didn't think that they would take a body and put it into the ground. So I went to my mother and said: 'You shouldn't bury him, the grubs will get him.' The very thought of the grubs getting my brother horrified me. That was my first real brush with death and I had nightmares for ages after that.

Both my mother and father had white fathers and black mothers. My father's father was a German and my mother's father was a Scot. When my mother's father died my mother was treated like any other black with a skerrick of white blood, living with blacks— she was rounded up and put in an institution. That was the law in those days, and at the age of ten she ended up in a home in Brisbane for uncontrollable Catholic girls. She was ripped away from her mother and never saw her again.

My father's mother had died of TB when my father was two and his father married again, a white woman. So we were the unmentionables.

Although mum was taken in by the Catholic Church at an early age they never bothered to teach her how to read or write.

28

She could quote the Bible backwards, but they never bothered to teach her how to read it. When mum met dad he was an oysterman and they met when he was on one of his trips looking for oyster beds and mum was on holiday. She was an inland woman and when she saw the sea she nearly had a fit. She had never seen a crab and it was ages before she could even look at a crab, let alone eat one. She thought they were the ugliest things she had ever seen. But I remember her as always being there with the food. She looked after our bellies and our warmth, and was always there when we needed her. She knew nothing about the white man's madness, because of her inability to read, so I wasn't as close to her as I was to my father because he had had a white education and he had a few answers which my mother did not have.

On Stradbroke we lived in a gunyah, which had bags all around and canvas whenever dad could get any. Then, when the government was ripping down the penal settlement of St Helena they gave iron and timber to dad. 'If you can do anything with it, Ted, it's yours,' they said, so he shipped it across to the island and put up another house for us. That house is still standing on Stradbroke today and I was about fifteen years of age when he put it up. I helped to put the roof on it.

Childhood I remember as a completely happy time. We were always on the hunt and it was a beautiful, happy, Aboriginal childhood. I even got something out of the white school system. We had one teacher, a Scot whom we used to call 'Old Schooly Mac' who didn't give a damn what colour you were. His job was to get the three Rs through your head, and he succeeded in doing this more than any other teacher I remember. I was a very lazy pupil at school. The only time I ever came top of the class was when Schooly Mac (Mr McPhail) offered us a prize of five shillings for the person with the top marks. I won that five shillings. I needed it and I got it. Apart from that I just mucked about at school.

I must say that I was anti-system at school—not anti-people, anti-system. I couldn't understand why, as I was a natural left-hander, I had to write with my right hand. To me it was a denial of natural rights. Nature had given me this gift and I didn't want anyone to take it from me. I was rapped on the knuckles every day with a heavy, round ebony ruler. I remember the day I gave in. My hands were so sore that I just couldn't pick up the pen in my left hand any more, so I went to the right hand. I remember the day I came home and accepted the fact: I stole my father's tobacco and I went behind his boatshed, rolled my own and smoked it. I remember it was Log Cabin and in a round tin. My father never knew about it. I was five!

Well, that experience not only made me anti-system, it made me anti-people at the time, even anti my own people. They told me I was mad. Give in and write with your right hand, they'd say. My brother, who was also a natural left-hander, when they told him he had to write with his right hand just shrugged his shoulders and did it. He had no hang-ups. Not me! I fought it, and what I got out of that school experience which I might not otherwise have had was a knowledge of conservation. I didn't know it as conservation then, of course, but my reaction to that experience made me seek friends among the birds and the animals. I knew where every bird's nest was. I knew where all the wild ducks lived, and where they laid their eggs. I knew all the quampees and the cowries and the cockles. I knew where they all lived out at high-water mark. I used to go out there and use my left hand where no one could see me. This was when my mother was always complaining to dad that she never knew where I was. After school I'd just disappear. I didn't play with the other kids, because they were always teasing me about being so stupid and stubborn. They could never understand why I was copping all these hurts all the time and not giving in. So I was anti-people at that stage, and I just lived in a world of my own—I shut everyone else out.

I think that even as a child I could not accept that the discrimination and intolerance we experienced was a fact of life that could not be changed. I think I always believed that there had to be an Australia where the Aboriginals took their rightful place at the same level as any other race in this country.

In my Aboriginal education I learnt a lot from the old grannies. When my father got married he had to move away from the sitting-down place of his parents to a new area to make his own camp, so that the old camp wouldn't be crowded out. The nearest gunyahs at the old camp were about a hundred metres apart, but it was feared more would lead to overcrowding. So when dad was of marriageable age he and his generation had to find another place to live and they settled at the One Mile, which is a mile away from the old camp. Well, later on we children had the job every Sunday of going back to make sure that the grannies were looked after. We had to chop up their tobacco, peel the vegetables, get their water and get their wood. This was our Sunday job. And it was also part of our education. They used to tell us all sorts of things about the Aboriginal culture. I remember the grannies in the long, silly skirts the missionaries made them wear, with horrible starched dickies. They were also issued with shimmies and bloomers, but we knew, although the missionaries didn't, that the grannies wouldn't wear those things underneath. None of the missionaries ever investigated to see if they were worn, and in any case it was more convenient for them just to wear the dress. When we used to go out to their camp they would have the open fire in their little huts and as the grannies talked to you they would stand in front of the fire with their dresses hitched up so that they could warm their bums, which is a very logical thing to do. That was where I got my Aboriginal education, as had my father, who had also been educated by the old men who were still handing down the knowledge to the young people in my childhood.

One thing that happens when you've got a bit of white blood in you and have had a bit of white education is that when you misbehave people will say, 'Aha, that's the Aboriginal in you.' And when you accomplish something they will say, 'Aha, that's the white coming out in you.' It happened to me as a child and it still happens to me. People still think that what I have done is because I'm not a full-blood, that it's the white blood coming out in me, not the Aboriginal. I think these crazy people are utter racists. They think this because they don't want to feel inferior to me; it's psychological and they say it because I make them feel inferior; I don't purposely do it, but they do feel inferior. There are some people in Australia who have to have blacks in a certain place, otherwise they get fouled up in their minds.

My father hated racial discrimination and he used to say to us, 'Whatever you do in that white world just don't do it *as well—* do it *better than!*' He pumped that into us. And I am more like my father than my mother in that I inherited that determination. He could carry his knowledge so well, because in the early days of the island the whites, who classed themselves as superior, were nothing when it came to an emergency. When it came to bringing a boat across the bay in an emergency they would turn to my father and the men of his age who knew that sea like the palms of their hands. It was very galling for him when, like his two white step-brothers, he wanted to be a coastal captain on the little ships that sailed the area in those days. Now Howard Ruska is *Captain* Howard Ruska; Frederick Ruska is *Captain* Frederick Ruska, but because my father had the touch of the tarbrush in him he did not get into that field. That was very galling for him, not to be able to make the grade because he was black. My father never told me this—the old grannies did. They said, 'Teddy is a very clever man. Pity that they look at his blackness the way they do.'

These days I am living back on Stradbroke at my home, which I call Moongalba , where I run a holiday camp for kids. I've had over 8000 children visit me there in the last five years. I think children should be taught now, because they're the men and women of tomorrow. And furthermore I'm sick and tired of talking to mentally constipated adults; they don't listen. It's the children who are going to change this world for the better, not the adults.

When the children come to Moongalba I teach them the same way as I teach my own grandkids. I teach them how to pick up shellfish and where to look for them. I teach them how to fish and how to crab. I teach them what's good to eat in the bush and what isn't, and I teach them how to cook food under the ground. We talk about the cultures of all the different races and, having travelled all over the world, I've picked up a bit of art from each of the countries and taken them home and the kids can sit there and communicate through touch with these artifacts. One mother asked me if I was afraid that the children would break them; I told her that if they do I'll go back to the particular country and get another one! What the heck! Children are losing a very important part of growing up by having to go to museums and look at things through glass. How can they appreciate art if they have to see it through glass? There must be that touch of the arts. And nothing has been broken at Moongalba.

Moongalba is where I want to stay now. I could survive there even if all the white food and artifacts were taken away. I say to the children who come: 'I hope you know how to survive when they dig that uranium out of the ground. I know how to survive, I hope you do. Aboriginals have already learned the art of survival. They're the only ones who won't go down.'

This is my land: I have always said that, even as a child. The white people used to say to dad: 'That girl walks this land as though she thinks it's hers.' Dad wouldn't say anything. He'd just walk home and tell me, 'Mrs So-and-so said you walk this land as though you think it's yours.'

'It is mine, isn't it?' I would say. And he'd say:

'Yes, girl. Don't ever forget it.'

Jim Killen

The Honorable Denis James Killen has earned the right to be known as a self-made man as much as anyone has. He left school at thirteen to make his own way in the world, and after working on country stations around Queensland milking cows, fencing, dipping sheep, shearing, mustering and breaking-in horses, he enlisted in the airforce, where he served in aircrew.

He went to the University of Queensland and graduated LL.B. He joined the Liberal Party and was foundation president of the Young Liberals' Movement in Queensland. From 1953 to 1956 he was vice-president of the Liberal Party in Queensland. In 1955 Mr Killen was elected Member of the House of Representatives for the Queensland electorate of Moreton. In the 1961 Federal Election he retained his seat on the distribution of Communist Party preferences and in doing so saved the Menzies Government from electoral defeat.

From 1969 to 1971 Killen was Minister for the Navy and since 1975 has been Minister for Defence. He is famed for his eloquence in Parliament and his erudite classical exchanges with former Prime Minister, Gough Whitlam. He performs his parliamentary role with vigour but without malice or rancour towards his political opponents and is generous in his assessment of those whom he respects but with whom he disagrees. He wrote a glowing tribute in the introduction to Fred Daly's book From Curtin To Kerr. *He wrote: 'For my part, when I went to Canberra I never expected to find friendship with Frederick Michael Daly, but that is just what I have found. He is the wonderful epitome of the sentiment: "He that can be a worthy enemy, will, when reconciled be a worthier friend."'*

I was born in Dalby in Queensland on 23 November 1925. My father, James Walker Killen was a dentist practising in Dalby. He suffered mildly from asthma and he had come to Dalby from Victoria because it was recommended that he live in a drier climate.

My father died before I was two and I have no recollection of him whatsoever. My mother has never talked about him, other than to always impress on me his insistence that I always be well-groomed, clean and acceptable to people.

I remember once going back to Dalby and seeing the parish priest there—a magnificent Irish character, Monsignor Nolan, who had buried my father—and I asked him what my father was like. He said that he strongly suspected that he was very much as I am. He loved a drink, loved people, loved to have a bet and they're characteristics (some may not accept the view that they're qualities) that I have very much. He was most meticulous about his personal appearance.

I was entirely brought up by my mother. She described me as representing thirteen years' hard labour! The significance of the thirteen is that that was the year I decided to fend for myself and ran away from school. They must have had a pretty impoverished opinion of me because they didn't bother to put an ad in the Lost and Found columns! I went to the bush.

Mother was very ill at the time, she was left with a messed-up estate, there was literally no money in the house and mother had to take in boarders to make ends meet, and in those days there was very little in the way of social services and no pension. She made her own way, looking after my sister and me. I was at Brisbane Grammar School and I felt that I could make do for myself so I left and got a job working in the bush for a pound a week and keep.

I suppose I resented others having access to some of the comforts of life and some of the *indicia* of a comfortable existence that I didn't have. For example, I never had a push bike in my life. I never had a scooter. On Saturdays in Dalby I'd get seven-pence—sixpence to get into the pictures and a penny to spend.

I once bought a half share in a homing pigeon and I thought I was a person of very considerable property. The pigeon disappeared and I felt absolutely diddled about that.

I started school early at the Dalby State School, with the approval of the authorities, because my mother took the view that I was difficult to get on with. (Some people hold that view to this day!) I came back the first day protesting about the presence of Aboriginals at school. I was promptly taken back and that afternoon I brought two of them home to have a drink out of the waterbag. From then on they were among my closest friends.

I got into an extraordinary number of fights, as you can see by a nose that's all over my face. I played football, although I was a bit on the light side. I got some dreadful thumpings. I used to run—had to on occasions to get away from people. I think the general view was that I was difficult to get on with, a rebel, hard to manage. This was probably a fair assessment and not to be unexpected of a young person without any paternal control.

My relationship with my mother was very close and is very close today. I ring her every day in the week, no matter where I am in the world. Some may say that's a bit of an imposition on the taxpayer—well, so be it—the taxpayer makes a few impositions on me and I think it is the least I can do. She lives on her own.

My mother is a very proud woman, fiercely so. She wouldn't take assistance from anybody and certainly wouldn't ever ask for assistance from anybody. I admire her enormously.

I think I have learned or inherited from my mother a fierce sense of independence. I am not aware of having asked anybody for a favour, materially, in my life. I'd much rather walk ten miles than put myself under an obligation to anybody to get me there. Fiercely independent! Always have been and I like to think that I'll see out my days that way. So I have that above all from my mother, and a sense of pride in it too. I know that the fact that she would never, ever ask for help has made an indelible impression on my mind. If people wanted to give it to her in some unostentatious way, then so be it—but she would never ask. I also have loyalty from her. She was fiercely loyal to my sister and me. It could have been convenient to have been otherwise. From my childhood experiences I think I have also got a sense of humour—the ability to laugh at oneself and further to that, to laugh when there's been misfortune, to say, 'Could it be possible that things could get worse?' and shrug.

We moved from Dalby to Brisbane about 1934 and I went to the Brisbane Grammar School. It was a pretty substantial burden for my mother to keep me there—to pay the fees. I did tolerably well at school and at primary school my *forté* was maths. That strength has disappeared! I can't even make the slightest pretence of understanding the metric system today.

There were no discussions of politics at home, but I argued furiously at school in a very untidy way about what governments were doing. I was, I suppose, a little more articulate than a lot of people. I've a very clear recollection of the headmaster leaving my primary school and I was picked out to make the presentation to him. I can see the scene now, with the whole school there and me as bold as brass. He had a saying on school parade: 'If your head is still your body is still.' I remember as a kid of eleven taking him off. He took it in great spirit—and I guess I was a little precocious in that sense.

When I left school at thirteen I recollect another headmaster who was very upset and remonstrated with me. But I just left and went bush and that was it. I never had any sense of misgiving or any sense of uncertainty. I thought I was made, of course, with a pound a week and keep. I managed to get together a few little possessions by way of clothing. One of my great triumphs was saving up enough money to buy an alarm clock. I had to get up early and I felt that I was dependent on someone else's alarm clock, which was something of an affront, so I got my own. On some properties I'd be up before breakfast to milk ten or twelve cows, separate, wash up and get the horses in, and do all that before breakfast.

I read a lot in the bush, because I felt a very real sense of the inadequacy of my own education. I used to listen to the characters who lived in the bush. Argue with them. Even tell them to shut up from time to time! I was brought up in an environment there working with people with fiercely egalitarian views. They were wonderful people and I enjoyed them immensely. Life had been pretty rough and tough to them.

There was no corporate body of political dogma adopted and forced on me but even then I had political ambitions. This was sharpened a lot when I later went into the airforce, but it wasn't until the war years that I knew what type of politics I was going to pursue. Before that I didn't say that I was going to be a member of the Liberal Party or the Nationalist Party or any party. It was an inchoate gathering of political sentiment.

I remember the Depression and the arguments as to how it should be settled. I've got the clearest recollections of people that were down and out coming looking for work, any work to keep them going. I've got a very clear recollection of people camping in little humpies on the river bank. People with their clothes in tatters. I suppose that could have influenced one's social attitude. I've always been resentful all my life of unfairness. I don't resent a person disagreeing with me, but I resent being treated unfairly.

I've been in Parliament twenty-four years and I can't recall in that time many members whom I've actively disliked. I can recall two, and that's not bad out of hundreds. I've never said anything ungenerous about the two whom I disliked; I've just held my own private assessments of them. I think you can fight your political causes and do so with a measure of generosity and at the same time treat people with dignity and respect. Now where does that come from? My mother is always courteous to people. There are little things that still live with me today. She said that no matter how poor you are, as long as your fingernails and shoes are clean you can get by! She also used to say: 'Be courteous to people no matter what they do.' I don't deny for one moment that doing the job such as I'm doing you work under great tensions and that maternal injunction may be lost from view, but I like to talk to everybody from the gate-keeper to the Governor-General in the same way. I dislike immensely the term 'VIP'—this is a 'VIP' flight, this is a 'VIP' room. Every person in this world is important to somebody. I call the VIP Lounge the 'Courtesy Lounge'. If I walk across a floor that is being polished by somebody I excuse myself. I think it makes your existence a lot happier if you can act in that way, just to treat people as they are. I got that really rubbed into me when I worked in the bush, because there I met a lot of what I regard as the very great character and the very great strength of this Australia.

Religion played an important part in our home. My mother is a very stern Anglican and my father was a Roman Catholic. I have a very deep personal commitment to tolerance in the field of religion. I was christened in Dalby and confirmed in Brisbane and as a youngster went to Sunday school and church, although on occasions I'd wag it from Sunday school and turn up riding a horse somewhere. I don't attend church as regularly as I should, according to the Dean of Brisbane, but I confess I talk to God with growing regularity. I find it difficult to observe formal religion in my existence, which is a pity. It's an indictment I serve against myself that it's not always possible to be as punctilious about these matters as one should be.

I have three children, all girls. In applying some of the things I have learned from my own experience I've always insisted they be courteous, clean and seek to be tidy. I've had some spectacular failures with respect to the latter! They don't always share my political preferences. My eldest daughter, Diana, not infrequently says to me, 'Where on earth did you get that pettifogging idea from?' The youngest girl, Heather, has got very decided political views with an insistence upon having a greater tolerance of conflicting views than most people. The middle one, Rosemary, wouldn't have any emphatically defined political views other than a sense of fairness and justice to poor people who are incapable of fending for themselves. I see this as a concomitant to my own views. You'll notice the qualification 'people who cannot fend for themselves'. I take a pretty rugged view of people who seek to impose on others when they can jolly well make do themselves. I distinguish that in a flash from people who are absolute humbugs. The person who is physically, mentally or socially incapable of helping himself must be helped. I think the corporate strength of the community must be devoted towards that. I'm resentful of people of property and power imposing on the community, taking the view that the community owes them a living. The community owes them nothing of the sort. The community owes them the opportunity of making a living, but not of providing a living for them.

Clearly, we live in a completely different society today from when I was a child. Today there is material advantage offered to children, which, to me, would have been breathtaking. You only have to look around to see that. Far be it from me to offer any views, condign or otherwise on the contemporary generation. I think there's a lot very wholesome there, but I find myself pretty intolerant of some of the coarseness and I trust I'm not being patronising. I don't think that manners count as much as they did in my day. I notice a big difference in manners—to help women in and out of cars, proper table manners. Mother was very insistent upon that. Little things like walking on the right side of the footpath, addressing people properly; these things have always been very important to me and I don't think they're observed today with the same sense of *punctilio* with which I was required to observe them.

Pat Lovell

For fifteen years from 1960 to 1975 Pat Lovell was known to Australian children as 'Miss Pat', the friend of 'Mr Squiggle' of the ABC television show of that name. Ms Lovell had started work with the ABC as a typist who couldn't type and as a filing clerk. Since moving from behind the scenes to the screen, she has appeared as a panellist in Beauty and the Beast, *as an actress in several dramas and as co-compere of the* Today *show on Sydney's Channel 7, a position she filled for five years from 1969 to 1974. But in 1973 she embarked on a completely new career—film production. In that year she became co-producer of the very successful film,* Picnic at Hanging Rock. *In 1975 she produced* Break of Day *and in 1976 the thriller* Summerfield. *In 1979 she began work on* Monkey Grip, *a film based on Helen Garner's prize-winning novel.*

Ms Lovell is a part-time commissioner of the Australian Film Commission and is on the Advisory Committee of the Women's Film Fund.

I can remember, even as a child, never being able to understand why we couldn't make our own films in Australia. When I was about eight years old I saw Shirley Anne Richards, who was a star of some of our films of the 1930s, when she was making a personal appearance with one of her films. I can't remember what the film was called, but I was really overwhelmed by the experience and thrilled that we had our own film star, and that she really looked like a film star. So while I was at school it was a hideous shock to discover that we had no film industry as such, apart from little bursts of films over the years, and the Chauvels bravely carrying on.

I was born in Sydney in 1929 in the depths of the Depression, which had its effect on our family life. My father was an optometrist, and he'd set himself up in business and had spent a lot of money on equipment. At the same time my younger brother was extremely ill and the family had to have a full-time nurse. The costs were absolutely exorbitant and father's patients weren't forthcoming with their payments. He went bankrupt. But fortunately my grandmother won second prize in the lottery and saved the day and the family lived again. I think she went off for a holiday to Noumea and my father paid his debts and we were no longer under that particular cloud. We were under many clouds when I was a child, but that one remains with me.

Ours was a very sad household because my brother died. He suffered from a fat intolerance—I'm not sure of the name of the disease—but he had a complete intolerance to anything with fat in it. He went to endless specialists and it was a bit of a struggle. My other brother and I were constantly having to be quiet at certain times of the day and, because my father had his rooms at the front of the house, we weren't allowed to make a noise in the back of the house. But we did have a very big lovely garden at the back with everything in it and every tree was some sort of house and there was a lot of make-believe going on.

44

I had a third brother. He died two days after I was born so I was born under some sort of a shadow in what was not a happy house at all. He had pneumonia and was very ill all the time that my mother was in hospital with me and I think that for her first-born to die when she was in hospital having another must have really hit her for everything. In fact I didn't know all the circumstances until some time later. I used to be shown photos of him when I was little and would be told that it was my brother Peter and that he died before I was born. Then, ages after, when I found out exactly when he had died, I finally realised that he died, in fact, two days *after* I was born.

This wasn't the end of it. My mother had two more daughters and one of these died with a hole in the heart, so literally, out of six children, she has three surviving, and that must knock you about a bit.

She is a remarkable lady, because she still managed to spend a lot of time with us when we were little, and we always had stories read to us at night. I can remember that she always encouraged us to play—to be able to amuse ourselves. We lived in the western suburbs and the back garden, with the high paling fence, seemed to be our boundary. I didn't have many friends—a few here and there—and we had to make games up among ourselves. My mother used to supply us with all sorts of raw materials for those games. I remember in the back of the garden we had a huge old garage, and as we didn't have a car, the front was turned into a sort of workshop for my father and I managed to turn the back of it into a theatre of sorts. I used to bore people to death with various plays I put on there and mother always supplied dressing-up clothes or paints for me to paint backdrops and things like that. She was marvellous at making costumes and I remember at one stage she made me a Snow White costume which was beautifully made. I know I have never made my children costumes with such detail. Somewhere I also have a photo of myself and two of my brothers, in which I am dressed as a fairy in yellow crepe paper with tinsel round my hair and one of my brothers is a Chinese— complete with make-up. We were encouraged a lot to make the most of our imaginations.

My father used to help us with the make-up, and I believe he was quite a good amateur actor. I didn't ever see him act because I was forbidden to go to a play in which he was performing because I had put my brother's teddy bear in the wash-house copper! I can remember that very distinctly because it is the worst punishment that was ever meted out to me, I think. I had seen the sets, because they were hanging around the house, but I was not allowed to go because I had been fairly revolting.

My father was a marvellous man and I loved him dearly. He was also one of the most annoying people I think I've ever met. But he encouraged us in many ways. I remember we had the most fantastic birthday parties because he would make cakes and decorate them in the most amazing way. He was quite a good cook and would come up with wonderful things that we would have at parties. I can remember that up to my tenth birthday I always had a marvellous party. He was also very good at playing games with us and he spent quite a lot of time with us. I think he spoilt me a bit because I was a daughter. I think that he, like my mother, was desperately upset by my older brother's death and then by another brother's death, and I think he then transferred a lot of affection to me, which was very unfair on my younger brother. I remember my father with great affection.

I went to the local public school in Campsie and I remember very little about it because I hated it like blazes! I loathed it; loathed and detested it. All school means to me now is the smell of incinerators and sweaty bodies and hot asphalt and trying hard to learn things that I really didn't think had any importance. I remember the relief I felt when a polio epidemic hit Sydney and we were sent out of the area because it was very, very bad in the western suburbs. My father sent us all to Cronulla until the epidemic had passed. I remember I had not completed my homework and how lovely it was to be whipped out of school and taken off to another school.

I was always fairly devious about trying to do the least amount of work at school to get by. I was fairly good at school and used to come home with fairly good reports, but it was all a bit of a sham because I know I didn't work very hard.

Both my mother's mother and my father's mother were very strong women. My father's mother ruled the household with a rod of iron everytime my mother went off to have a baby. If one put one's hand on the dining-room table after it had been polished, all hell would break loose. This wrath didn't happen when my mother was around. My paternal grandmother in fact probably brought me up and influenced me greatly in the early years of my life. And even though she was a dragon, she was a kind dragon and quite an amazing lady herself. She had been sent out from England as an orphan to Australia when she was eleven, and so she had had quite a stormy time. She was an extremely independent woman, and I think I have probably been more influenced by the women in my family than by my father. As a child I thought my father was the stronger character, but in the end he was not at all. I bless my grandmothers because they have made me very strong. This has meant that I've been able to cope with things that other women may not have been able to cope with and they have given me a certain fighting spirit.

From this grandmother I got determination as a trait. She'd been deserted by her husband who'd whipped off to Fiji and was killed in a hurricane. It was all very dramatic and she was a most attractive woman even when it happened. But her moral code was really something to be reckoned with. Her code of behaviour—the way one behaved when one was with other people—was strictly something left over from the Victorian era. It was always 'Sit up straight, Patricia,' and 'Stand when people come into the room.' It stood me in good stead when I went to Presbyterian Ladies' College.

My parents were very strict with us as well and my father told me later that we were very well-behaved, but then we didn't get much of a chance not to be well-behaved, because we were punished—very severely. I can remember being whacked very thoroughly. Both of them believed in taking a brush or strap if necessary. I took my brother out for a walk once and lost him—I think it was on purpose. When I got home I really did get the hide tanned off me.

From my mother I learned to appreciate literature and poetry, because she read to us when we were very small. I remember once she was reading us *The Jungle Book*, and we were all crying because it was terribly sad. My poor father came out, after seeing some patient, and he hit the roof. 'What're you doing to the children?' And we're all saying that we like it! So my mother influenced me a lot in appreciation of words and later, when I went to boarding school, one of my chief escapes was to go into the library and read so much poetry that I almost drank it. I probably got through a whole lot more literature, especially romantic literature, than a lot of other kids the same age. It was an escape for me.

I fantasised all the time as a child. I can remember being accused of lying when I was ten, but I was actually fantasising about something. But I was pulled into line and told that I must learn to know what is truth and what is not. I think I did this because I was terrified of tragedy. When my younger brother died I remember my mother telling me, or discussing it with me, when we were coming home on the train. I'd been sent off to stay with somebody and we were coming home on the electric train. (Those wretched trains go right through my childhood. Every time I get on one now I sort of go back to square one again.) I remember she told me about my brother and I was so desperately upset, but I didn't want to make a scene on the train. I didn't want to do anything in front of other people or break down. I remember hearing her say to somebody afterwards that I was very heartless, that I was not moved, when I was almost destroyed by it. I was really not very fond of the present, and I think that's probably why I used to play all these games where I was anything but me. That fantasising lasted a long time, right through school.

When we left Campsie I was sent off to board at Presbyterian Ladies' College in Armidale. That was even worse than primary school and I cut up there a hell of a lot.

My parents split up and my father married again when I was about sixteen. The marriage had been on the split, as it were, probably from the time I was about nine or ten. I used to try and ignore it and pretend it wasn't happening because I loved them both very much and I wasn't prepared to let it happen. But, of course, it did and it was exceptionally upsetting. I was visiting my grandmother when my father told me that he was getting married again. I remember coming back on the ferry and informing him that I felt the best way to die was to go over the end of the ferry—which worried him more than somewhat. I had some marvellous fantasy that diving into all that foam would be a way out. It wasn't meant as any blackmail at all, but I hoped to get through to him that I wasn't feeling very good about the whole thing.

I can remember some of the things that were going on in the world around me when I was a child. I remember very distinctly the abdication of Edward VIII. I came home from school and my mother was crying and she was making me a dress—white voile with pink roses. I came in and stood behind her—she had one of those treadle sewing machines. She was so upset. I can also remember the outbreak of war and the H.M.A.S. *Sydney* going down, because one of our friends was on it. I distinctly remember the dropping of the atom bomb on Hiroshima. I was at boarding school and we were all called in in the morning by the ministers of the various denominations and we were shepherded in to see them. I was absolutely appalled and confused when told that this bomb that had destroyed thousands of people had been dropped for the good of the world. I just couldn't cope with that at all. I asked questions like why wasn't it dropped at sea, but none of these was answered and I was in a terrible vacuum about the whole thing. There was no real elation at all. I think that was when I first started to question right and wrong. That was the awakening of any critical ability I have, because until then I'd been a sponge—taking everything in and not really querying anything.

I went to a Church of England Sunday school when I was little and when I was about eight or nine I brought home one of those forms that said I had to swear for the rest of my life that I would not drink or smoke. My father was absolutely livid with rage about that and removed me forthwith from the Church of England Sunday school. My mother said that I had to go to Sunday school, regardless, and when the Presbyterian minister came around and had a glass of sherry with my father, I was sent off to the Presbyterian Sunday school. My father used to say that he was an agnostic, and he and my mother used to have big rows over religion.

I'm a loner, there's no doubt about that, and I think I got that from my childhood by being thrown back upon my own resources all the time. I'm also fairly pig-headed, which probably came from being a daughter in a household of boys, as I was for a while, and wanting my own way all the time. As a film-producer I'm also a bit of a risk-taker, which is strange, because I don't think I got that from my childhood. I've never been a gambler. My father was. He played the horses, and one of my worst childhood memories is of hearing the races on Wednesday and Saturday afternoons. We had to be quiet and if father won, everything would be pleasant; if he didn't, it would be sheer hell. Now, the minute I hear

50

the races being called, off goes the radio. I can't abide it. It's anathema to me. So I don't know why I'm a risk-taker—that's something that's just evolved over my life.

My marriage split up in 1968 and I made the big decision to take my children and leave, which was a hell of a risk to take. Having survived that and survived it exceptionally well, it gave me confidence that I didn't have before.

I have reflected on the fact that in our family there have been three generations of broken marriages and my ex-husband made me reflect on it all the time. He used to say to me, non-stop, you'll never be a stable woman because you've come from a history of broken homes. He doesn't know it, but the reason the marriage lasted thirteen years was because I was determined that it would not happen to me. It was not my mother's wish that her marriage break up; in fact it was a disaster for her. Mind you, I don't think it was my grandmother's wish either, although she must have been a fairly horrendous lady to be married to. I don't blame grandfather for going off to Fiji and finding himself a nice little place, even though he came to a rather sticky end in a hurricane.

I married somebody who I thought would give me the stability that I needed. He was older than I was and he came from an extremely stable, settled home. I thought that's what I needed. It's the biggest failure of my life and one that I'm very ashamed of, that I was not able to make that marriage work. It saddens me greatly. I was very determined to make it work and I think I gave it a good try.

Finding a connection between my present work in film-making and my childhood is easy. I remember many films from my childhood, both in a good and bad way. There are still things that scare me when I recall them from my Saturday arvos at the movies. I remember one particular episode in the Phantom serial where he was thrown into the flames, locked in a coffin. At that stage I thoroughly believed that heroes needn't survive—that they weren't

51

absolutely invulnerable. I thought that was the end, and I went home terribly upset about it. The other thing I saw which terrified me—I don't even know why I was allowed to go and see it, because my parents strictly supervised everything we saw—was *The Mummy's Hand*. This terrible mummy got up and walked around the pyramids strangling people. If I want to feel terrified I just have to think about that. But the first film that I saw that I really loved, my mother took me to see. It was *Pygmalion* with Leslie Howard and Wendy Hiller, and I absolutely adored it, which in turn got me reading George Bernard Shaw, which was marvellous. During the time I was in boarding school we didn't go to the movies, except during the last two years at school when I used to come down from Armidale for the holidays and do three sessions a day. Then I really got to love movies more than anything else. One film that sticks in my mind because I have seen it at least ten times, is *Les Enfants du Paradis*, the film of Marcel Carné. That, to me, embodied all that should be in a film, and it put all my childhood fantasies together and put them on the screen, and that was amazing. As soon as I left school I joined a film society and saw things like the Flaherty documentary *Nanook of the North*, and then, going right back, *The Cabinet of Dr Caligari*, *The Battleship Potemkin* and *The Italian Straw Hat*.

I also used to listen to the radio a lot, mainly to music. The good thing about boarding at Presbyterian Ladies' College, Armidale, was that because I hated it so much I got to listen to some very good music and read poetry. That was the best thing that could have happened. It started as a defence and then it became an absolute joy.

One thing I regret from my childhood is that I didn't continue to learn ballet, which I started when I was nine. I was very lazy. I had decided that I was going to be the prima ballerina but I didn't think practice was necessary. When I was a child I wasn't a stayer at anything. I think at one stage my mother thought that I would never stick at anything and when I stayed in television for seventeen years that surprised her and convinced her that I would stick at something I could get my teeth into. But as a child I was inclined to flit around. I also had a fear of people, and it was only when I was doing the *Today* show on television that I overcame this fear of going into a room where I didn't know anybody. I would much rather walk away. I'm still not good at parties. I hate them. I'm really terrified if I hear people talking behind a door and I have to go in through that door. The *Today* show helped a bit, because in the early hours of the morning I would have to go up to perfect strangers, quite often famous ones, and say: 'Good morning. My name is Pat Lovell. Can I ask you some questions?' That did me a lot of good and I think without it I would never have become a film producer.

My happiest childhood memories are of Christmas mornings. Waking up in the dim light and my brother and I sneaking out of bed and grabbing the presents, because I always knew there wouldn't be any arguments on Christmas Day. My grandmother would also be nice to us when we'd go across to Neutral Bay for lunch with her. Even in the 103 degrees (39 C) heat I would have to put on my best clothes and we'd get the train and ferry to go over to Neutral Bay and Christmas Dinner. One would have to '. . . sit up straight, Patricia!' and all that, but it was still a good day because everybody was happy and relaxed. My mother and father didn't fight. My grandmother was even nice to my mother, which was rare. That was when I was little and it was great fun. Later it became a bit much because we had to go to the other family at night—rather like the Bruce Petty cartoon of Christmas Day in which the whole family is lined up against the wall, a map is spread out and the father has a stick which he points and says: '9 a.m., nuts with Aunty . . . '

I have two children of my own, now twenty and twenty-two, and I've tried to bring into their childhood the good things of mine. To be close to one's parents is very important. My mother literally spent all her time with us and had no time to herself whatever, but when mine were little I used to work once a week, because I thought it was very necessary for them as well as for me, so long as they were well looked after at home. It has paid off, because I think they were always happy to see me when I came home and they were not neglected in any way whatsoever. For things like birthdays I think I followed in my father's footsteps. I gave my son a pirate party once which was a hoot. I remember I stayed up four nights until 4 o'clock in the morning making swords out of cardboard and silverfrosting them. That was a lot of fun, and I knew that it had given my father and my mother a lot of fun to have those games with us.

I'm probably much more open with my children. We've always discussed problems much more openly. I hope they haven't needed to fall back into fantasy as I used to. I hope life's been good enough for them not to have to do that, because that leaves a lot of my early life very fuzzy and possibly retarded my development or maturity. I've tried to make living more palatable for them, facing up to the facts of life and making the best out of it. It can be a joyous experience, you know.

Bob Hawke

Robert James Lee Hawke is the son of a Congregational clergyman, born in Bordertown, South Australia, on 9 December 1929. In 1952 he was West Australian Rhodes scholar and spent two years in Oxford doing research. From Oxford he returned to the Australian National University to do work for a doctorate.

Bob Hawke has been president of the Australian Council of Trade Unions since 1970, a position to which he was elected after having served as the ACTU's industrial advocate and research officer for some years.

With his belief that the trade unions' sphere of interest should extend beyond purely industrial matters, Hawke has involved the ACTU in service stations and petrol distribution, retailing and travel, through ACTU-Solo Service stations, Bourke's Store in Melbourne, and ACTU Jetset Travel Service.

Because of his advocacy of the Israeli cause he has been honoured with a tree plantation named after him in Israel.

From 1973 to 1978 Hawke was federal president of the Australian Labor Party. Since 1972 he has been a member of the governing body of the International Labor Organisation. He has been a member of the Reserve Bank since 1973.

In 1979 Mr Hawke was made a Companion of the Order of Australia for his services to trade unionism and industrial relations.

I was born in Bordertown, South Australia, in 1929, a fact which excited one extreme Left interjector at a trade union meeting to yell out: 'And the bastard's been sitting on the bloody fence ever since!'

My father is a Congregational minister, and the Congregational Church is not a denomination which has much paraphernalia, so the overt signs of religion in our home were limited. It was a home in which grace was always said, but there was nothing very significant in that. In the years as a child in South Australia we lived in a place called the Manse in small country towns, so in that sense it was identified as a religious home, but I would think if anyone had come into either the home in Bordertown or in Maitland he wouldn't, by any visible sign, have known that it was any different from any other home.

My father is a great man. I think he's one of the best human beings I know. In the whole of the time I've known him I can't remember any occasion in which he's been guilty of anything mean, or anything which hasn't been a practical reflection of his faith in the brotherhood of man. I mean that in a quite practical sense with nothing sloppy about it. In a very real sense he reflects his belief in the fatherhood of God in terms of what it means in the brotherhood of man and I think he's just a very good human being.

My father, and the Christian religion which he has always practised, have had a very significant influence on me. I don't embrace the Christian faith now, but the sort of principles that I've referred to which he reflected in his life have certainly influenced me. I hope that I have essentially the same attitude.

I can remember a few incidents from my early years in Bordertown, where we lived until I was five. I can remember one occasion when Dad was driving me somewhere around Bordertown in the car and the door flew open and I fell out. I did no damage to myself but I can remember Dad being terribly worried and concerned about me, and telling me not to say anything to my mother because she'd be terribly worried. Nothing very significant in that, but I can remember it quite clearly.

I must have had some sort of propensity for declamation at an early age because I can remember there was an old lady associated with the Church who couldn't get around very much and I used to go down and stand up on a box in front of her and preach sermons to her. It was regarded as a little bit precocious! But even with this precocity and the fact that I loved my father and was proud of him, I don't remember ever thinking that I would be a minister.

We went to Maitland in South Australia when we left Border-town and I can remember a lot about it. It's the centre of a farming community and Dad had not only the church in Maitland but he had some churches out of it. They were not really in towns, they were perhaps just the church and a school together in one place. He used to travel out into the farming community a lot. I liked going around with him very much in that sort of environment. I remember staying on farms and enjoying it. Once Mum and Dad went on a long car trip to the eastern States with a couple of people who were in the church and for that period I lived out on a farm and went to a tiny little school. I thought that was marvellous and they were happy, happy days. There was a great sense of security attached to it all.

I had a brother who was nine years older than myself and he died in 1939 of meningitis. It absolutely broke my mother up and when Dad got the call from a church in Perth I think one of the reasons he accepted it was that they wanted to make the break from the tragedy of that event.

During my formative years my brother hadn't lived at home—he'd been a boarder at King's College in Adelaide and I only used to see him occasionally on holidays. When he died he'd finished at college and was working in Adelaide in the public service. It was a different sort of relationship than normally exists between brothers, in that I lived with him very little, so his death may not have been the same awful tragedy it may have been in other circumstances. Of course, I remember being terribly, terribly sad—and seeing what it did to my parents, there was a vicarious sadness from that too.

Moving to Perth for me as a young boy was an enormous adventure, going on a train all the way across Australia. Looking back on it subsequently it obviously was a big thing.

My mother was quite a dynamic person and very much involved in issues. Probably the greatest influence she had on me was instilling into me the importance of education and of working hard in that area. The scholarship that was taken at the end of the sixth grade, the last primary school year, was very important in Western Australia because it determined whether you got into Perth Modern School or not. It was a scholarship that was sat for by nearly all the kids in the primary school system and I can remember Mum instilling into me the importance of winning a scholarship. She used to give me extra tuition and incentive and push in that period, and I think that the sense of the importance of education is something that has stayed with me. And I did win a scholarship.

I had my views on the importance of education later confirmed in a rather unfortunate way. I got the scholarship and was able to go through Modern School fairly easily. I didn't work hard. I was able to get a good Leaving result and get into university but I was nowhere near in top gear as a secondary school student. The first year at university I wasn't working very hard and during the second term holidays I had just got a motor-bike and was riding home, not feeling well, when I had a blackout. I had a bad accident and was on the critically-ill list. I ruptured my spleen and it was taken out. I was on the critically-ill list for the best part of a week and my life was very much in the balance. I can remember very distinctly that when I came through and I knew that I was going to live, I had a very serious think. I felt that my life had been spared and that I should now use it to the hilt, and that was reflected then in the way in which I approached my education. I sat for the exams at the end of that year obviously under considerable difficulty. I hadn't been able to work for weeks and weeks and I had one of the exams deferred. I got fairly ordinary results, but I'd made up my mind that I was really going to apply myself and I did and I've always done so since. So the attitude that in an initial sense had been put into me by my mother was very strongly reinforced by that experience.

Perth Modern School was an educationally elite school and it was co-educational, and I think that's obviously a good and very sensible thing. It was one of the few co-educational schools and it was regarded as the top school academically. It got the cream of students out of the system. Only the top fifty people in the State got scholarships and the next fifty got what they called 'entrances'. So you got a hundred students going in there each year, who—apart from some who went to private church schools—were the top academically. That standard of student was also reflected at the teacher level in that it was regarded as the top school within the State system, so you had a combination of able students and top-class teachers and co-education. It was a very fortunate environment. The school also had excellent sporting facilities and very spacious grounds. Perth Modern School was recognised as a school of academic excellence and very considerable opportunities, and I derived advantage from it. I'm not necessarily arguing that that's what should happen in education now. I think the important thing is to provide within the education system a breadth of facilities so that no child, wherever he has to go to school for geographical or other reasons is going to be disadvantaged. If you've got good facilities for everyone *then* there may be some arguments for an institution where you're going to give some sort of accelerated opportunities to some. But the important thing is to have good opportunities for everyone.

Politics was always a subject of discussion in our home, even in the pre-war days. Of course, when we moved to Western Australia it was more so because Dad's brother, Albert, was then a Labor

Member of the Western Australian Parliament. He went on to become Premier. He had a country electorate, the seat of Northern, and he lived in a flat in Perth while Parliament was sitting or when he was working in his Minister's office. He used to spend quite a deal of time with us. I would think he came to our home at least once a week for a meal, and so it was inevitable that in that context politics was talked about quite a bit. I admired my uncle and he certainly influenced me. It would be too much to say he was a hero, but obviously I was very proud of him.

I was always encouraged as a child to have my say. I was never conscious of any feeling that I was to be seen and not heard. I was encouraged to read and to discuss what I read. I was encouraged to read newspapers and to understand what was happening. That fact, of itself, was important. At school there were debating societies and I was active in them. I even once led a debating team against another led by John Wheeldon! So at that early stage at school I was interested in the process of argument.

Within the church I was very active in the youth organisation and became president of the young people's association in the Church of Australia. I was very active in church affairs until I was in my early twenties. In fact I was an Australian delegate to the World Conference of Christian Youth in South India at the end of 1952. I think that was the beginning of the end of my beliefs in organised religion.

The conference was held in Kattayam in the State now known as Kerala. It was the state with the highest level of literacy in India and this was because it had a greater penetration by the Christian church—both Catholic and Protestant—than any other state. One of the results of that was that the Communist Party was stronger there than anywhere else in India. I remember there was extraordinarily cheap communist literature at communist bookstalls in the area where we were. I couldn't help contrasting the blatant opulence of the church and the leaders of the church, and the totally unrealistic price of Bibles and Christian literature, with the fierce dedication and involvement of the communists. It didn't persuade me to communism but I can remember one day there the hierarchy of the church put on an enormous garden party in one of the big homes. There were delegates from all over the world and there were impoverished people really looking over the fence at the people gorging themselves. On Christmas Eve there was a party, again put on in one of these big homes, and we sang carols and hymns. Two lines that stuck in my mind at the time we were singing were the lines: 'Christ to the world we bring, The world to Christ we bring.' It all seemed like so much irrelevant and hypocritical nonsense to me. I walked out of the party, thinking about these things, and went down into the streets where there were scores and scores of people just lying in the gutters asleep. I was sickened by the hypocrisy and irrelevance of it all, which is not, perhaps an entirely rational way to begin one's disaffection, but it nevertheless operated that way with me.

My childhood was basically a very happy time. Not long after we went to Western Australia dad became a chaplain in the army so there was a dislocation there while he was away. He didn't go overseas, but he was not living at home. We had other people living with us for most of the time he was in the army. But I was always surrounded by great love and affection and security. I never knew what insecurity was and I had enormous encouragement within the domestic environment and there was always a great deal of pride in any achievements that I had. I don't think anyone could have asked for more.

We never had wealth in any sense, but again there was never poverty. While I was conscious of the fact that other kids at school had more material things than I had, insofar as things that I really needed were concerned I never had any problems.

I loved sport, particularly cricket. I was a cricket fanatic and quite good at it. I was in the 1st XI at school before the final year.

I played in the 1st XI in my fourth year and then in my final year. In my first year at university I was playing first-grade cricket and one of the decisions that was associated with the accident that I talked about before was how intense I would be about sport. I think that if I hadn't made the decision to go to the extent of my ability academically I might have put even more into cricket. I played first-grade cricket all the time I was at the university and in the winter I played baseball and also a lot of tennis. Sport was always something that I enjoyed and was reasonably good at, and it gave me a range of friends beyond what you got in other fields.

I have three children of my own, one son and two daughters. One thing that emerged out of my own experiences as a child was that I was determined to encourage my children to develop whatever talents they had as much as they could. From a very early age I urged them to do as well as they could, not simply to derive parental pride out of saying 'There's my kid, look how well he's done' (although it would be dishonest to say that you don't get that pride out of your children doing well), but I knew from my own experience just how important to me doing well academically had been. I totally enjoyed my work as ACTU advocate and research officer, it opened up enormous vistas for me and I wouldn't have reached that position unless I had done well academically in law and economics and gone on to Oxford. I knew that the happiness and enjoyment and fulfilment that I was getting out of life was very much related to the fact that I had utilised to the full the capacities that were within me. So it was important to me that my children should stretch themselves. In no sense am I sorry that I tried to do that.

Associated with that was the conviction that I wasn't going to try and tell them in what direction they should go, because in my own experience again the final path of my career was something that took a long time to emerge. I was a sort of professional student for a long, long time as I did law. When I finished my law degree I worked for a very short time as a trainee executive with an oil company. I got enough money then to go back to university full-time and do economics. Then I got the scholarship to Oxford and was there for a bit over two years and then came back as a research scholar at the Australian National University. Even when doing a doctorate at ANU I still didn't know what I was going to do in terms of a future career. Then, in a sense quite out of the blue, came the offer to go full-time to the ACTU. I was twenty-eight then, so I realise how futile it is to be trying to say to your children: 'Look, make up your mind what you're going to be!' My real concern was to try and ensure that they gave themselves the best opportunity to equip themselves so that whenever the time came that they did want to make some decision they wouldn't be looking back and saying: 'Bugger it! Why didn't I do that? That's an opportunity I've foregone.'

Bob Ansett

Robert Graham Ansett is the son of Sir Reginald Ansett and his first wife, Grace. When his mother and father were divorced and his mother remarried an American, Ansett went to live in America. He returned to Australia when he was thirty years of age to establish Budget Rent-a-Car of which he is managing director.

Bob Ansett was born in 1933. Although still an Australian citizen he was drafted into the US Army at the time of the Korean War and trained as a paratrooper and was to be assigned to the 187 Airborne Division. However, he was so good at football that he was assigned to a football team in Japan and never went to Korea. He says: 'The Far East Armed Forces Commander wanted it to be the best football team ever put together, so all we did was play football in the winter months and I ran the swimming pool in the summer months.' He was offered three football scholarships to American universities and selected one to the University of Utah in Salt Lake City.

After leaving university he took up a number of jobs in marketing and merchandising in California. Having become an American citizen after his discharge from the Army he became involved in politics and in 1965 'played a minor role in the San Diego area of the Barry Goldwater campaign.' He vowed that if Goldwater lost the election he would return to Australia.

His company, Budget, was a small latecomer in competition with Avis, which enjoyed the monopoly on airport service throughout Australia. When Ansett Transport Industries acquired Avis, relations between Bob Ansett and his father became very strained. That monopoly has now been broken, although Avis still enjoys a significant advantage in airport operations due to the refusal of Ansett Transport Industries to lease space to Budget in their terminal buildings at some airports.

I was born in Hamilton in Victoria in August 1933 at the time when my father was establishing his business in the Western District. My mother comes from Maryborough, which is not far from Hamilton, and we lived in that area until I was about four or five. After that we came to Melbourne and lived in Hawthorn for a couple of years before my father bought his property at Mt Eliza, where we lived for a couple of years before he and my mother were ultimately divorced.

My mother remarried, marrying an American who was an engineer with Lockheed Aircraft, and my brother and I, who were eight and ten respectively, went with my mother and step-father back to the United States. We lived in Los Angeles for the next five or six years. My brother, when in his teens, came back to live with my father but I stayed with my mother in America.

I sometimes look back on my parents' divorce and find that I honestly don't have any strong recollections of it. I think that it was a time in my father's life when he was terribly busy developing and building his company, so I guess we didn't see a great deal of him anyway, and my recollections are that the break-up of the marriage wasn't any great trauma.

Probably the dominant adult in my childhood years was my grandfather, my mother's father, who lived in Maryborough. I spent a great deal of time with him and I seem to have had very strong recollections of his influence in the first ten years of my life. He influenced me by cultivating interests, particularly in sport and a little bit in reading. He was the Maryborough Town Clerk and on the week-ends he used to take me to his office and introduce me to reading and sport, both of which are very important to me.

My mother wasn't a particularly strong influence on me. She is a very vivacious person with an enormous personality—a very attractive woman and, probably because of these components in her make-up, she had a lot of varied interests and I don't know that children were a major one. Her second marriage ended in divorce but she still lives in San Diego and I see her once a year. She's a very self-supporting and strong-willed individual.

For my schooling I went to Wesley College in Melbourne and in the final three or four years before I left Australia I was a boarder, so again I was separated from parental influence. It was a different time and age. It seemed to be something that happened very regularly, particularly with people from the Western District, that the kids were sent off to Wesley or Geelong Grammar or Melbourne Grammar. In our case, too, it was a little bit difficult because it was about the time we moved to Mt Eliza and I don't think there was much in the way of schools down there at the time and the roads weren't particularly good. It was a long drive from Mt Eliza to Melbourne. I know that my dad even had an apartment in Melbourne because it was a very tedious thing to try to drive it each morning and night. But still, with my children, there was no way that I would consider sending them to boarding school. My parents had very little influence on me because of that. I'd only see them on week-ends or during holidays and even then I seemed to spend most of the time with my grandparents. When I was told that we were going to America it sounded terribly exciting. I didn't particularly enjoy boarding school and I guess I looked forward to breaking out of something of a strait-jacket.

I've always been a person who likes to do my own thing in my own time and I found boarding at Wesley pretty restrictive. When I went to the United States, after being there about a year, I ended up going to what they call 'a military academy' near Los Angeles and again it involved boarding and was very much more regimented than Wesley. It was a military environment, and one that I don't think is good for any child at that age to be sent to. You had to wear a military-type uniform from the moment you got up in the morning until you went to bed at night and you had to drill with simulated rifles even at the age of ten or eleven and you earned rank. I ended up a sergeant in the two years I was there. When I say I didn't particularly enjoy these experiences I didn't dislike it or anything, but I found it restrictive.

Neither my mother nor my father were very strong influences on me in the first ten years of my life, yet there are quite strong similarities in characteristics between myself and my father, which must be genetic. I don't think it was an environmental thing.

I remember my father in the time of my childhood as a very strong personality and I think 'swashbuckler' would be the best word that pops into my mind. He seemed to be always on the go. He was an attractive person, very strong-willed. Obviously he'd set himself an objective and he was working towards it. One of the very earliest memories I have of him is of his running a limousine service to the Victorian country areas, and I remember accompanying him on many of his drives when I was about four or five, and he was a very fast driver—or seemed to be at that age. Then when he got his first aircraft I was introduced to flying at a very early age and that was something that I got a great sense of adventure and excitement out of.

When I came back to Australia I had just turned thirty-one and while I had seen him from time to time in the United States during that twenty-year span and we'd write to one another occasionally, I guess it must be thought of as a very distant relationship. He didn't particularly discourage me from coming back to Australia, but he didn't encourage me either. I understood that when I returned whatever I did was going to be self-generated and I wasn't expecting any sort of support from him. So when I came back we met one another for drinks and lunch occasionally, and then over the next thirteen years, the time I have been back in Australia, the relationship tended to develop into an adult friendship. It was certainly not a father-and-son relationship. He gave me some very helpful business advice from time to time and it's been that way ever since. I suppose because of the fact that we came into direct confrontation with one another, with his company buying our major competitor, and the Court challenge to the airport monopoly that his company was in a very strong position to secure, we've crossed swords a few times business-wise and that must affect your personal relationship. I think at the moment you'd have to say that things are fairly cool between us. I hope that when this quietens down and the airport contract is behind us that things will revert back to what they were previously, but I think we're both pretty strong-willed people and I saw his move into rent-a-cars as a threat to my objective, and I've responded the way that I would have assumed he would expect me to respond: as he would have responded.

I'm like my father in being strong-willed, and I think also in my dedication to the achievement of objectives—the will to win. He wasn't a particularly good athlete, but I think I was. I had that will to win as an athlete and that held me in very good stead and had an enormous influence on my life. Even the things I do today have their genesis from my training as a sportsman, particularly a team sportsman. Now, while my father didn't participate in sports he always had a will to win, and I think that genetically that is something I acquired from him.

From my mother I inherited certain personality characteristics. I'm more of an extroverted person than my father is and I don't think I take myself too seriously. I think he takes himself a bit more seriously than I take myself. I can laugh at myself and I don't hold any long-term grudges. I think I'm a pretty easy-going sort of person, although I'm still the sort of guy who wants to succeed and wants to win and I'll do what I have to do to do it, but I don't think I'd ever be described as 'ruthless'. He has been described that way. I don't necessarily define his business practices as ruthless, but then others do seem to.

I first met my step-father when I was about nine and he spent a good deal of time with me in the period between ten and fifteen, very important years. I didn't have a close relationship with him and he was a different sort of person to my father and I thought he was a fairly weak character. For the first couple of years he took a fairly close interest in both my brother's and my schooling and personal development, but that ceased about the age of twelve and he had no influence on me from that period on. After I got older we didn't particularly hit it off. And his marriage wasn't a particularly successful one, either. It broke up by the time I was about sixteen.

At the time I went to America, which was in 1941 or 1942, I was aware of the things that were going on in the world around me. I get back to recollections of my grandparents, because I think that is where I became aware of the world. I'd listen to the radio broadcasts on the ABC every afternoon at four o'clock. Then, when we went to the United States, we went on a Swedish ship. Sweden was neutral, and we were confronted by a Japanese submarine on the way over. It surfaced about a mile from the ship and there were communications going back and forth and it was a pretty exciting experience and of course brought home very clearly the fact that a war was going on. Even though I was only ten years of age I knew what it was all about.

Looking back on my childhood I think the thing that I didn't have that I wanted to ensure my children did have is the right level of communication with their parents. I don't think that I've ever had what I would consider to be a proper communication with either my father or my mother, and even now I find it very difficult to communicate with her. With my father it's a slightly different set of circumstances, because any sort of communication is directly business-related. Now, I didn't want my children to grow up that way and not be able to communicate with their parents, so I tried very hard to avoid that. I encouraged them, when they had problems or needed assistance, to see that their parents should be the first ones to approach, rather than to try and sort it out themselves. There are pluses and minuses in that. I guess I've been a very independent guy since the age of twelve or thirteen. In my final year in high school my mother moved to San Diego and I wanted to remain in the little town of Vista to finish my last year. I was playing football and involved in all sorts of things, so I moved in with another family for that final year. After that I went off to other parts of the United States and to Alaska on my own. So I've really been on my own since the age of fifteen. While I wouldn't want my children to be that way it didn't do me, the final product, any harm. I think because of that I am able to deal with adversity or deal with particularly difficult challenges better than I would otherwise.

I must say that I had a good learning capacity and didn't have a great desire to work as hard as I should have in school. I think I got by on basic commonsense. Now, being able to identify the effort that my younger son is putting in and the success that he is getting in school, and thinking how I got through with basic intelligence without working at it, that I do regret. For some reason I just didn't see it as a challenge. It was when I'd gone from the structured environment of boarding at Wesley and the Military Academy at the age of thirteen into a co-ed high school that there was an enormous change. At that time I lost interest in the academic side of school and got involved in all the peripheral activities of American education. They have all sorts of social things, much more than we do in Australia, and one of the things I particularly enjoyed was public speaking. That was something that I was introduced to in America—the ability to communicate and project yourself to a group of people. I didn't have that in Australia, but in America the instructors try to get all the kids to lose whatever inhibitions they have and that is an enormously important thing. That's one thing where I've always been able to compare the Australian and American education systems, and that is to me a very vital thing. American kids, from kindergarten on, are more articulate than their Australian counterparts and it's mainly because they have no inhibitions in expressing themselves. I particularly enjoyed that in America.

Americans, at a very early age, learn and have a great respect for their country and I think that they go to great extremes to sustain that respect right through their lives. The people themselves, and this is a broad generalisation, like to be involved in many things. The average housewife and the average youngster will get involved in politics, as I did. They get involved in theatre acting and in community affairs—they just are involved people, a bit more than Australians are. I think that we have become a little bit insular. I lived in one of the outer suburbs of Melbourne after we returned to Australia and I was staggered at the fact that people, particularly the women, seemed to have no interest outside of looking after their home and their children. In America, of course, that's not so. I like the way Americans really get behind something as a community. It all comes back to the school. I can remember when my first son went to kindergarten, on his first day he had to stand up in front of the class and tell about his family, what he does on the week-ends and so on. You start off that way, communicating to groups of people, and they are interested in your personal activities, or you believe they are.

I took a great deal of interest in American history at school and I believed completely in the private enterprise system and I felt that the Republican Party epitomised the private enterprise system more than the Democratic Party. My first involvement with politics was with Dwight Eisenhower. I got out of the Army just at the time he ran for a second term and I voted for him then, exercising my newly-won right as an American citizen. Then I got more involved with the Republican Party and I got involved in the 1964 Presidential campaign, playing a minor role in the San Diego area of the Barry Goldwater campaign. This interest in politics also came from school. In high school they have a student council and even in your first year you have representation on that council. Each year selects

74

its representatives in an election held along exactly the same lines as an American presidential election. You have campaigning and a convention and parties, although they're not called Republican and Democratic. Even in my first year I stood for office and was elected, and all through my high school years I was an office-bearer. The whole democratic process appealed to me and I took a great deal of interest in it. We had the whole hullaballoo, signs all over the campus, all the electioneering slogans, you stand up and give talks to gatherings—as I say it's a vital part of the make-up of most Americans and it's an enormous introduction into the democratic system. You've got to win on your personality and your projected abilities. There are council meetings once a week and a president of council is elected. Ultimately you have representatives who attend the city council meetings. Of course in America you don't have compulsory voting and they rely strictly on the citizen feeling a responsibility to vote, and not just in the Presidential elections because in America they elect everything from the dog-catcher to the local sheriff and the judges. The system wouldn't work unless you have a political awareness at a very early age.

My three children all have varying personalities, but one has become very reliant on me. He's now twenty and he's in Hawaii working for Budget Rent-a-Car and I'm hopeful that the separation will make him a little more self-reliant. I said to him, before he went, that really the greatest risk you can take is not to take a risk at all. That's certainly not an original saying, but it's one that I've been aware of most of my life, and I think it tends to reflect itself in lots of things a person does. The things that I learned, from playing football in particular, I've translated into the way I run this business. I've tried to develop a team environment and I've tried to do the things that I think a successful football coach would do. We're a highly motivated company even though we're geographically dispersed which doesn't make it easy. I've tried to instil the will to win into the employes of the company and I think in a service industry those things are very important, and that dates back to this early introduction to team sport and taking the risk. American football is a body-contact sport, much more than Australian football, and perhaps the one attribute that I had over others in the team was that I always had a personal disregard for my own safety. My only interest was in winning the game, and I would do whatever was possible. This has always been part of my make-up. In the paratroopers, jumping out of aeroplanes, I've never had a great personal regard for my own safety. Even skiing down mountains people can't believe the dumb things that I do. I again relate this back to my son, who has a better physical co-ordination and could have been a better athlete than I was, but lacked that dedication and desire and will to win. He grew up in a more stable, secure environment. There are regrets that I didn't have that sort of growing-up factor, but on the other hand I would have been a totally different person if I had.

My two younger children are different and I think maybe I tried a little too hard with the eldest one, being a boy, than I did with the other two. We sort of moderated it a bit with them and they are more self-reliant. So you can go to extremes, and when I think back I think I probably overprotected him or was overly concerned about that communication and didn't give him enough opportunity to become more self-reliant. But that is probably the biggest thing I tried to introduce in my relationship with my children—to be involved with them a bit more than my family were with me and it's not always that easy. I've developed this company from zero base in thirteen years and it is absorbing and involves a fair bit of travel, but still I think I've compensated to a point and we're able to do things together and that's good.

I think I'm able to hold some sort of balance between family and business. They're both very important to me, but perhaps the business is more important than it ought to be. That's a genetic influence, I'm quite sure of that. I get an enormous satisfaction out of achievement and that requires a great deal of my time, but I don't think that my family's been disadvantaged as a result of it. For example, I make it a point when I take an overseas trip to take one of the children with me, so I think that in that sense I don't ignore the importance of the family. But I'm sure if I didn't have this business and I was a nine-to-five guy working for someone else there would be a different attitude toward the family.

The fact that my mother had two unsuccessful marriages made me want to work harder at my own, and I might have overcompensated as I did with my children. My parents' divorce didn't leave any scars and I wasn't hurt emotionally by it. But I am also now in my second marriage, so you might draw some conclusions from that. My first wife and I returned to Australia with three small children and I got involved in a totally new environment and in a great deal of travelling in building the company and it changed the relationship between us. After about six years in Australia our marriage failed. I remarried about three years ago and my children stayed with me, which was a mutually agreed thing. I think my wife felt that as the marriage had broken up she wanted to be completely free to lead a new life and from my point of view I felt somewhat guilty at the break-up of the marriage, because I had changed, there were no two ways about it. I felt that if she wanted to start life anew then the least I could do was take on the responsibility of the children. And at that time, when the eldest would have been about sixteen, it suited me because I wanted to maintain the relationship with the children and so I was more than happy to take on that additional responsibility.

My childhood, I guess, is divided into three parts: the first part was in Australia; then an interim period in the United States, for about three years of which I was in a strange environment, going to boarding school again; and then the final third, which was at the high school in a small town. The happiest period of the first third of my childhood was living at Mt Eliza where my father had bought an enormous property, 100 acres (40 ha) and very rough and rugged. It was real country and he had a farm. He had buildings all around the place, chicken hatches and things. We used to go rabbit hunting and I learned to shoot a rifle when I was about eight or nine. The time at Mt Eliza was *the* highlight of that period in my life. In the next third there were no highlights. I don't think going to a military academy is good for any child. I don't have any emotional distraughtness about it—I just didn't enjoy it. But in the final third of my childhood my personality developed. I felt that I was a popular guy at school. I was an athlete, I was vice-president of the student council in my final year and was involved in all sorts of school activities. I really enjoyed my four years in high school and as a sustained period those years were the most enjoyable of my childhood.

Anne Deveson

In 1974 Anne Deveson was appointed a commissioner of the Royal Commission on Human Relations which made its report in 1977. But she is not quite as well known to Australians as 'Commissioner' Deveson as she is as 'The Omo Lady', a fact which she considers unfortunate, because the Omo commercials represent two days' work a year, while the work on the Commission required her constant attention for three years.

Ms Deveson is a journalist, film producer and member of the New South Wales Anti-Discrimination Board. She is also on the Council of the Film and Television School and a Governor of the Law Foundation of New South Wales, a research and educational trust fund for the legal profession in that state. She has written Australians At Risk, *her personal observations on the work of the Royal Commission on Human Relations, and is the producer of a number of television documentaries on social issues. She has also made three films for World Vision, one during the famine in Ethiopia in 1975 and a more recent one on the plight of Indochinese refugees in camps in Thailand. The third was made in Uganda in 1979 immediately after the overthrow of Idi Amin.*

After doing a science course at university in England, she took a job as a trainee copywriter in an advertising agency, and from there moved into journalism. Under assignment to Associated Press she became one of the first western journalists to enter Albania after the communists took over there.

In 1958 she returned to Australia, where she had spent several years as a child, experiences which she describes here.

At the time I was born, in 1930, my father was a rubber planter in Malaya. I was born near Kuala Lumpur. When I was two we returned to England, so I remember nothing of those early days in Malaya.

My father, who was a man of many moods, decided that he didn't want any further separation from us as a family and that he would try to make a living in England. Unfortunately the Depression was not a good time to make a living. He bought a hotel in London, but he didn't know very much about running hotels and after a year or so he went broke. I think this was partly because he used to feed his guests on lobster and strawberries, and that's not a very sensible way to run a business. Eventually he had to go back to Malaya and my mother and brother (who is three years older than I am) and I stayed on in London. I didn't see my father again until I was about six and later, when I was ten, when we went back to Malaya. He was virtually a stranger to me when we met again in 1940. He had become very concerned about us when the war started, particularly after the Battle of Britain began, and I can remember a period of frantic telegrams passing to and fro. He felt we would be safer in Malaya and eventually the three of us went out there, straight into the arms of the Japanese.

After we arrived there my father, who loved the country very deeply and had considerable communication with people at all levels, had some inkling that there was going to be trouble, and my brother and I were sent to a boarding school in Perth. My mother flew out on the last plane that left Malaya and my father, who was in the Volunteer Police, had a remarkable escape from the Japanese, but he was very ill when he arrived in Perth.

My mother was very much the dominant parent during my childhood. When it was clear that the hotel wasn't going to work she went out to work. She was a remarkably talented woman who had considerable artistic ability. She had been to the Central School of Arts and was a designer. She designed fabrics and millinery for a lot of the film people. She was a very courageous, vital, gay person who liked things happening around her. I think she was a person who was great fun to be with. She was enormously resilient and no matter what happened she always used to pick herself up, and do it with considerable humour as well. I was very close to her and I had a lot of fun with her.

I also had a period in my childhood when I had the traditional English nanny. When we had returned from Malaya we took on board one of those indomitable nannies, complete with uniform, who was very distressed because she really felt she'd come down in the world. She'd been working for an Admiral of the Fleet before she landed with this very broke ex-colonial family who couldn't afford anything better than a cane pram! We never had one of those great big 'Rolls Royce' sprung prams and I can recollect nanny being very upset about this. She had a big influence on me because of the fact that she was always there, a very stable element in what otherwise might have been a fairly unstable childhood, because we were always moving.

We didn't stay long in London. When I was about six my mother, being a romantic, decided that the London air was too foggy and not appropriate for us and that we should move to the country because what she really wanted was a simple country life. She bought a Queen Anne farm house in Buckinghamshire and we all decamped down there, but of course she didn't really want a simple country life at all. She used to enjoy the weekends and going for walks across the fields, but I think she missed the vitality of London and her work. She also missed the income because my father, back in Malaya, was having difficulties supporting virtually two families. So she returned to work as a buyer in the fashion industry. She could bluff herself into almost anything and got a job as a millinery buyer for a big complex of stores in England, with branches all over the country. She hadn't had any experience, but she was an extremely creative person with a lot of confidence in herself. From then on she lived in Liverpool, where she was based, and travelled a lot through Europe and America, buying. She used to come back at weekends, so, with my brother at boarding school, I was really left alone with nanny.

Nanny's name was Mary Rusted, and she'd had an incredible life, really like *Upstairs, Downstairs*. She'd been 'put out to service' when she was thirteen and made to put her hair up and her skirts down and she was a very frightened little girl, I think, looking back on the stories she told us. She'd never married. She obviously invested all her emotional energies into the children that she looked after and really loved very warmly. She'd had many years working with the naval family and had obviously become deeply attached to the children and I think she found it very difficult to leave them and come to us. I think that whole era of the British Nanny was an extraordinary one in terms of the kinds of lives they must have led and the emotional involvements they had with children they then had to let go. She was full of maxims, such as 'Neither a borrower nor a lender be' and 'A stitch in time saves nine' and all those sorts of Victorian stoicisms.

I was really not conscious of having an unusual childhood, with my parents absent so much of the time, until one memorable day when I was walking through Kings Cross when I was working at the Commission I realised that I had always thought back on my childhood as being one which was very much the family round the kitchen table stirring the pot of soup, and it suddenly dawned on me that I'd never really had that. I think what was symbolic for security (and I had a great deal of emotional security as a child) came both from Nanny, who was always there, and from an enormous amount of warmth from my mother, who I always knew was going to be there. I knew that she came back on weekends and that when she did I would have cuddles in bed with her and go for walks with her and have fun with her. We also had a number of aunts, uncles and cousins around and there was a lot of happiness around the house, which I think is what had always given me the feeling that I'd had a far more conventional childhood than in actual fact I did have.

There is a blank in my childhood memories as far as my father is concerned. I have a few recollections of him when I was about two, as a very tall man of whom I was slightly frightened and who I can remember rejecting on a couple of occasions and being conscious of the fact that I was hurting him while I was doing it. Then when he returned on leave when I was about six I recall a very close time with him because he used to tell us stories. He was a very inventive person and used to tell stories about Bunny Matchsticks and I recall him from that period with a great deal of warmth. Then there was another blank and when I met him as a ten-year-old in Malaya he was a complete stranger and in a way I resented him, quite unfairly, because I thought that he had uprooted us from England. I think that must have been very hard on him because he was a sensitive person.

Now I would say that although I was closer to my mother, mentally I am more like my father. I think he was probably a frustrated academic who would have been much happier in a contemplative career. He read and thought a great deal, and was a person with a tremendous sense of the ridiculous with whom I was later to have quite profound conversations. He was a person with a wide-ranging mind, whereas my mother was inclined to flit, enchantingly and very happily, like a butterfly from one thing to another.

My brother was sent to boarding school when he was about nine, which was very much part of the English middle-class tradition. I think I would have gone to boarding school when I was twelve or thirteen if we had stayed in England, but as it was I didn't go to school at all until I was about seven. However, Nanny had taught me to read and when I was about three I was reading quite fluently and digesting newspapers when I was four, so by the time I went to school I actually had quite a problem in that I was way ahead of the kids of my age. From then on I tended to be put in classes with children who were about two years older than I was and I think that was a mistake. I really didn't have the same emotional maturity that they had. When we went back to Malaya I had a brief period at a convent boarding school there. I was in a class with girls who were two years older, but the nuns considered that I was too young to actually sleep with them because I might find out all sorts of things that I shouldn't, so I was put in the babies' dormitory and yet went to class with the others. Understandably, I really never had any friends, because the little girls that I slept with thought that I was far too superior because I was in the other class, and my class-mates thought that I was a baby.

I learnt very easily and quickly and I had the kind of mind that could absorb facts and spew them forth for examinations, which is not always a good thing. I had a great delight in learning in my early years, but because I was doing well in comparison with kids two years older I very early on got a label stuck around my neck that I was 'the clever one'. I think it's a great mistake to label children like that, because I felt that I had to live up to it and I became competitive and I really wanted to come top. Competition like that is a great destructive force in education because it leads to a great deal of inner anxiety on the part of the children who are involved in that sort of system. I don't think learning should be seen as a competitive event in which you either pass or fail. I think it should be something joyous that happens—that is a reaching out and extension of yourself. Furthermore, if we give prizes for academic skills I think that says a great deal about our kind of values in society, in that there are many other attributes people have that I think should be lauded and should be encouraged and fostered. It creates great divisions between those who succeed, be it at school or sport, and those who are regarded by the system as not succeeding and therefore as failures. We should look at the totality of the child or the person and not give them points for this attribute or that attribute.

I had an episodic reaction to school. There were periods when I loved it and periods when I absolutely hated it, was extremely lonely and didn't fit in very well. It was in those times that I particularly clung to any kind of academic success. I found the move from school in England to boarding school in Malaya very difficult to cope with, partly for the reasons I've mentioned and partly because it was a very strange environment. In those colonial days the only school that was considered suitable for the children of white personages was one Catholic boarding school and I can remember finding the exotic climate and the strange surroundings quite frightening. I remember lying in bed at night and seeing the rows and rows of mosquito nets looped around the beds with the nuns flitting back and forth with their cowls looped back. I can remember feeling that I'd been plunged into some extraordinary, unreal, bizarre sort of world and finding it very difficult to cope and being very homesick. When we moved from there to boarding school in Australia I again found it difficult. I think that one thing that my schooling taught me, because I moved to a number of schools, is a kind of resilience, in that I had to learn to cope with the teasing and the loneliness.

I spent a short time in an expensive boarding school in Perth, and after Malaya fell we went to the local State school. We were teased because we were English and there was a lot of antipathy to the Poms and Reffos. I was one of a whole gang of English kids going to this school, and we all took our shoes off and our accents became almost incomprehensible, even to Australians, because we were trying to fit in. We really became a tough, marauding gang of kids.

After Malaya fell and my mother had escaped to Perth we had no money and the Red Cross sent us and two other families out to live on a property that was about sixty miles (100 km) from Perth and was owned by an ear, nose and throat specialist who had decided to let refugees live on it as part of his war effort. We lived there for about a year. There were about eight children in the three families, and the three women, none of whom knew how to boil an egg, found themselves with a copper stove and having to grow their own produce. The school was 6 or 8 kilometres away and we had to go there by sulky. After a few abortive attempts to get the horse into the cart, at which it bolted and the sulky collapsed, we gave up. We never went to school. So I had a year of running wild, and that was just tremendous. We used to pretend to go to school, but I think the three women in their separate ways were extremely distressed. One was very ill and subsequently died of a tropical disease. The second one's husband had been killed in Malaya. And the third one—my mother—was pregnant in her mid-forties. This occurred as a result of my father being sent to us by the Red Cross for a weekend before being put into hospital. So all three of them were not very well-equipped and were finding it hard to keep afloat and to keep tabs on this motley assortment of children. So we really did run wild, and I remember that with extreme joy and exhilaration. It was a very good period.

I won a scholarship to Perth Modern School and had a year there which was great. Then, in the second year, my parents were thinking of going back to England which I found very disturbing. At that period I went through a very rebellious stage. I nearly got my scholarship taken away from me. I didn't work. I truanted from school. I generally made myself socially unacceptable, and I think that was because I was angry about the insecurity I was feeling.

During my childhood we moved from comparative wealth to extreme penury. My father was ill for a very long time after he arrived in Western Australia. He was in hospital and there was a long period when we had no money at all and were dependent on the Red Cross, who fed us, housed us and generally looked after us. When he came out of hospital and got a job teaching Malay in the army we had enough money, but only just enough, because we'd incurred so many debts in the earlier period when nobody was earning anything and we were always paying back. We were very much watching what we ate and we didn't have the money to have shoes mended. I remember wanting to go to the pictures and not being able to afford it. We were never literally starving but we were very broke. From then on and for quite a long period of my adolescence I was very conscious of money and the fact that we didn't have it. When we were repatriated to England when I was fifteen, and until I left home, we were extremely poor because neither my father nor mother could get a job. There were always tremendous worries, moving from one grotty rented house to another. My father had the habit of putting the bills that came in under the carpet because he was a tremendous escapist. So from about eleven years of age on lack of money figured enormously in my life. I know that there were times when bills came in and people felt sick inside because they didn't have the money and didn't know how they were going to pay them. I remember really suffering because of not having the money to buy clothes and to do the things that other kids my age were doing. For example, I can recall a dance—the first dance that I went to—and we were living in a reasonably prosperous suburb and everybody was buying their first long dresses to go to the dance. We just couldn't and this also affected the other two girls about my age who were living in a sort of extended family with us. We either had our mothers' cut-down dresses or we made them ourselves and we didn't have any sandals to wear, and I remember my mother made sandals for all of the three of us out of felt. Felt soles that she cut out and tied coloured tape around. They were great except that when we got to the dance they all fell to pieces! I felt different and I resented it. I can remember talking to a woman from the Brotherhood of St Laurence and hearing her tell of the damaging effect it can have on family relationships to not have enough money to live on adequately and to be constantly worried about money. It erodes family relationships if you are worried about the hole in the roof or whether you've got any money to buy shoes for your kids or pay the school bills. Unless you've been through a period like that I think it's difficult to appreciate. It can be very frightening to feel there's a big draught coming up your back door.

I can remember when we were living in Sheffield when I was fifteen or sixteen and our penury was such that my mother went to work in London, my father wasn't working and the family was scattered. My younger brother, who was two, went to stay with relations in Bradford and my older brother had joined the army. My father went into a boarding house in Sheffield and I went to stay with school friends to finish schooling. I used to see my father at weekends and it was agonizing, because I couldn't talk to him and he couldn't talk to me. I came across a letter he had written to my mother expressing extreme disappointment in this doltish daughter who never opened her mouth. It wasn't until I was grown up and could appreciate the reasons for his withdrawal and moods and he felt freer in his old age to reach out that we then began to establish a very good relationship.

The fact that my mother, from early childhood, worked and was independent and laid great stress upon economic independence affected the way I saw male and female roles. She had been through a period of economic dependency and it was obviously very important to her when she began to earn her own money. She and my father always kept separate bank accounts, which is something I've never felt the need to do, but I didn't grow up with the feeling that life depended on getting married. I grew up really conscious of the fact that you could take hold of your own destiny and do what you want with it and if you didn't like what you were in, well, too bad, you got out and moved on to something else. On the other hand I can recall my mother saying to me, after I'd been doing science at university for a year and hating it and not knowing what to do, 'Why don't you go and take a secretarial course so you can be secretary to some man with an interesting job.' I felt very angry and I can remember thinking, 'I want the interesting job.'

I don't mean that my mother never worried and didn't get frightened; she did. But she had this extreme courage and confidence in herself. She was the kind of person who, if something went wrong, wasn't going to sit back and let that swamp her whole life, because life was meant to be enjoyed, not lived in misery. She would literally up and change what was happening. She tended to be mildly intolerant of people who were not as resilient. And she was also very restless, which is a characteristic I can see in myself sometimes and I don't really want to be as consumed as she was by always having to do things. She was never a contemplative person but was constantly active. She'd be moving furniture at midnight, or sewing loose covers for chairs and making clothes and hats for people at all times. She did this when both she and father were out of work and sometimes she made a martyr of herself when she needn't have done.

There are some pluses from my unstable childhood. For instance, I enjoy travelling and it doesn't disturb me if I don't have anywhere to sleep at night. If I run out of money I always feel that I can find it again somewhere, or if I lose my bus ticket I feel it will be all right, it's not the end of the world. And I think that sort of ability to cope with change is a plus, for which I'm grateful. I think that another thing that comes through having a lot of change in childhood, painful though it can be, is that you learn how to make friends and how to open up to people. You have to go into a new classroom, feeling sick inside, and you have to go up to the woman next door and ask her where the shops are—in other words, you have to be able to open up communication with people, and I think that's a plus. Another was growing up with other children around, firstly on the property out of Perth, where the three families were living together, and later in Perth itself, the three families moved into a two-bedroom bungalow house and the kids all slept in the sleepout. That was a very good period, because that kind of extended family is really very supportive. You learn how to live with other people and you learn that there are others beyond those who are closest to you who can give you love and in turn take love.

Two or three years ago I was talking with Margaret Mead and she was stressing the need for children to have people other than their mother and father around, and for people to be able to expand beyond the very tight confines of the so-called nuclear family. Children need someone who can take them fishing and show them the stars—and this was something that I appreciated in the early adolescent period. The fact that there were the other two women and that there were other children around me, some older and some younger, and the fact that the three families had other friends and relations, meant that the house was always full of people. Sometimes, if you wanted privacy, it could be hell. But on the other hand I always had the feeling that there was someone I could turn to if I was feeling lonely, or if I'd had a blazing row with my mother. Children go through periods of being unable to talk with their parents, no matter how good the communication, just because of the fact that it is a parent-child relationship. It's very important that parents understand that and respect that need, and it's important for kids to have someone else—some other adult—with whom they are easy and friendly and can open up.

I would like to see both architecturally and in people's attitudes towards family life a recognition of the very positive things that can come from some sort of community living that means more sharing. It shouldn't preclude any kind of privacy, because privacy is important, but so is sharing. One of the things that concerned me when the Commission Report came out was the very hostile reaction to it that I think came about through people's fear of change. People criticised the Commission's definition of the family in which we talked about the need to recognise that a family can be many different groupings of people who are living together under one roof in a caring kind of environment. I don't think that's something we should be frightened of. We should be far more flexible and recognise that there are many different kinds of families and that families and children have different needs.

I have three children of my own and I think the values one imparts to children are not the things you say but the things you are. I think honesty is important between people, and I don't think I always have that. I was a very manipulative person, probably because of moving from one environment to another, and because I am the kind of person who wants everything to be happy and wants people to be joyous and life to be lovely. There's a very strong Pollyanna element, and I know for a long time I used to very much manipulate the environment in order to make it that way. I think that's a fool's paradise, so I think it's important with children to live with reality, which doesn't mean not enjoying fantasy, but learning to recognise that fantasy is fantasy. I think you can overprotect children from what's happening in a family. It's better to talk through problems and admit that they exist rather than try to cover them up and pretend they're not there or pretend that you're going to jump over them quite easily.

Warmth and affection and loving and touching are very important. I had that in my own childhood. I'm conscious of quite a lot of warmth and holding and demonstrativeness as a child and I feel that's very important. Unless you have that yourself you can't give it in return. I would like to think that I am free enough to express the feelings that I have, because otherwise you're a half-dead person and it's important with children to be able to show spontaneity with them so that they in turn are free to be spontaneous.

Charles Mackerras

Sir Charles Mackerras is one of a remarkable family of brothers and sisters who have distinguished themselves in a number of fields. One is headmaster of Sydney Grammar School, another is Australia's best-known psephologist, yet another is a lawyer and social rights activist, one is one of Australia's outstanding China specialists, one sister was a ballet dancer and another a musician. Sir Charles is the internationally known member of the family, having gained recognition as a respected orchestral conductor. He has conducted orchestras in London, Hamburg, Paris, San Francisco and New York. He was regarded as a child prodigy because of his ability to quickly master a variety of instruments. He was musical director of the English National Opera from 1969 to 1977, and has been Chief Guest Conductor with the BBC Symphony Orchestra since 1977. He has many outstanding recordings to his credit, including recordings of his own arrangements of the music of Sir Arthur Sullivan ('Pineapple Poll') and Guiseppe Verdi ('The Lady and the Fool').

Sir Charles was born in Schenectady, New York, on 17 November 1925, when his parents were living there temporarily while his father, Alan Mackerras, was working with the General Electric Company.

I returned to Australia with my parents when I was about two years old, so naturally I have no memory of my life in America. In fact, one of my earliest memories is of when we were living in Vaucluse, right at the top of a hill overlooking the harbour in Sydney. I can't say that the memory is either pleasant or unpleasant, but it was the sound of the bolts being hammered into the Sydney Harbour Bridge. From where we lived we could look over the harbour and see the two arches coming closer together and, even though it is miles and miles from the bridge to Vaucluse, I could always hear this crashing and banging. Perhaps it distressed me more than it might have other children because I was an incipient musician and my ears were more sensitive than others.

When the bridge was ready and finished it was very exciting for me to be allowed to sit on the roof—this was when I was about five or six—and watch all the fireworks that were attending the opening. After the bridge was opened, of course, it meant that the whole of the North Shore was opened up to city workers and, indeed, the Mackerras family moved out to Turramurra on the North Shore line, a very nice place. First of all we roomed there, and then we built our own house in Turramurra, which remained the family house until my father died.

My father was an intensely keen yachtsman, and of course Sydney Harbour is virtually the yachtsman's paradise. I was brought up very much with the yachts and sailing and the sea life (although the easy sea life, if you know what I mean). It used to frighten me very much whenever my father wanted to go outside the Heads, where the waves were particularly big. When we would occasionally cross the Heads one would feel what it must be like to be really on the open sea in a little boat. My father's was a thirty footer or less.

My father took yachting very, very seriously, and many of the rest of our family rather took against yachting because my father was so strict about it. You mustn't bring sand into the boat and

96

mustn't go in with wet feet and you mustn't do this and you mustn't do that. He took it immensely seriously, and of the family, as far as I know, the only one of the seven children that my father had that still likes going sailing is me. Being the eldest perhaps I was less affected by my father's strictness. Looking back I would say that, apart from music, memories of sailing with my father are the happiest childhood recollections I have. However, there was one thing that slightly spoilt all the sailing activities, and that is that almost all of us are very fair, very ginger-headed and of course that's not very good in the Australian sun. We were always having to cover ourselves up.

My father was a very modest man and I was never quite sure what he did, but I was told later that his main achievement in life was the extension of the electrical supply system in New South Wales. Later he became a senior lecturer in mathematics at the Sydney University, and also lectured in astronomy. He was a great amateur astronomer, and had a telescope through which we used to look at the stars and planets when I was a kid. It was particularly nice in Turramurra because it was so high up that one could get an unimpeded look at the heavens.

My mother came from a very distinguished Australian family—about which books have been written. She was descended from the first professional musician in Australia—a man called Isaac Nathan, who had come out to Sydney in the 1840s and had practised as a musician. His children, however, married into the medical profession, and had become doctors, and from then on in the generations the family was almost entirely medical. One of my ancestors, Sir Normand MacLaurin, who had come out to Australia as a ship's surgeon, eventually became chancellor of the University of Sydney. Those of his children who survived the Great War of 1914 were distinguished doctors, and my mother came from this medical and intellectual family.

My grandfather (that is, my mother's father) had been an early gramophone addict. He was also a great Wagnerian enthusiast. Because my mother had so many children I was frequently farmed out on my grandmother to stay with her at Rose Bay while my mother was having another baby, and I started fiddling around with the records and the old wind-up gramophone. These were the very earliest pre-electrical recordings of Wagner and Beethoven, and it was during these visits to my grandmother that I first realised that I was musical—that this was my main interest.

My mother liked music very much and my parents had a certain number of classical records. My father was a Gilbert and Sullivan addict and had all the Gilbert and Sullivan operas on recordings and knew the whole of them off by heart. He was the sort of person, fairly common in Australia, who hadn't really got further than Gilbert and Sullivan, which they regard as the whole basis of their culture. I knew the whole of Gilbert and Sullivan myself at a very young age, but I also knew a lot of Wagner, which may seem rather a strange combination. It is, in fact, a strange combination of interests shared by my brothers. My brother Alastair, the next eldest in the family and now the headmaster of Sydney Grammar School, has a tremendously wide, catholic knowledge of music, but I think that deep down the two composers he likes most of all are Wagner and Sullivan.

I had, in a way, my first musical experience with Gilbert and Sullivan because in Sullivan's operettas you can find in embryo all the devices which are used by great classical composers. There's counterpoint; there's interesting orchestration; all kinds of things that one sees in miniature in Sullivan's music which one also sees used to great effect by other, greater composers. At my first school I played the part of one of the fairies in *Iolanthe* and later took the part of Koko in the *Mikado*, and was said to be very successful in that. Then, later still, one of my first professional engagements as an oboe player was with J. C. Williamson's Gilbert and Sullivan season in the old Theatre Royal in Sydney.

My mother always alleged that I had a sense of musical style even as a child because once, in church, the congregation was singing 'Onward Christian Soldiers' and I said immediately 'Oh, this reminds me of the *Gondoliers*'. Well, it just so happens that Sir Arthur Sullivan did compose 'Onward Christian Soldiers' and my mother used to regard this as a great proof of my tremendous musicality.

My mother was the person who first gave me a sense of the importance of artistic things. She was crazy about historical matters, chiefly European. She wasn't really interested in anything nearer to Australia, such as the Orient, only European culture, and I really derived my interest in European things from her.

I started composing music at a very young age and I also, I must say, stopped composing music at a fairly young age too! I started when I was about ten and stopped in my early twenties. I composed all sorts of music, but I was mainly interested in the orchestra. When still quite young I had a book on orchestration by Ebenezer Prout who was a famous pedagogue in England at the time, and I tried my hand at orchestration. One of my early piano teachers, a student at the conservatorium, arranged for me to have a little chamber orchestra to try out some of my compositions. I composed in the style of Haydn and Mozart, all very derivative, and for a dramatic cantata, in the style of Handel and Purcell. This cantata was very successful actually, and was based on a libretto written by my mother on the subject of Marsyas, the musician of Greek mythology, who challenged the god Apollo to a musical duel, which was very suitable for setting to music.

I had started to learn the violin when I was six or seven at Pymble Sacred Heart Convent. As you probably know in Australia almost all musical life begins from the convent where nuns teach the violin and piano, not only to their girl pupils, but also to people who come into the convent just to learn music. A funny old lady, Sister Mary Lawrence, taught me the violin. She was rather over strict, so even though I liked the instrument I gave it up after a short time and took up the piano.

Learning an instrument came very easy to me and I also took up the flute. I bought a very cheap flute which was a good instrument but it was at the wrong pitch. It was what is called 'high pitch', which is nearly half a tone higher than normal and therefore didn't play properly with our piano. I soon realised that if I played everything half a tone down that it would play with the piano and this was regarded, I suppose rightly, as being an example of rather outstanding musicality in a tiny child. Transposing instruments in the orchestra is nothing to me because I had already experienced in practice playing this sharp-pitched flute with the low-pitched piano and having to transpose as I played.

I think musical ability is an innate characteristic. Mozart could compose when he was six and had already written operas of outstanding quality by the time he was fifteen and sixteen. I am not comparing myself with Mozart in any way, but the fact that I could do what I have just described, transpose by instinct, a task that others might work for years to accomplish, I think indicates that musical ability is something a person is born with. Some people are born mathematical geniuses—my brother, for instance, was always able to do extraordinary calculations in his head, which is a thing that I could never do. I'm sure that all these talents are innate, but at the same time you must work to foster a great talent, and that is what so many people today seem to me not to do. They have a terribly amateurish approach to their art. I find both in the pop field and the so-called serious music field too much is left to chance now and not enough is based on real knowledge of the art.

Having said that I must admit that things came easily to me and I was rather lazy. I didn't practise enough. I used to just rely on my innate talent, which used to get me into trouble. But it also helped me. After I had started to learn the flute I read in a newspaper that the orchestras were very short of oboe, bassoon and horn players and that very soon it was going to be difficult to provide Australia's orchestras with these players at all. So I thought, 'Ah hah! Here is a chance to get into an orchestra quickly.' I changed from learning the flute to learning the oboe, and I got a scholarship to Sydney Conservatorium and within a very short time I was playing in orchestras professionally.

That decision was made when I was about thirteen, against a lot of advice. At that time being a musician was considered a very risky profession, particularly among the professional classes. I was advised by many people to go in for one of the professions, such as law, and just regard music as a hobby, but I did not take that advice because I was determined that I would be a professional musician. My mother was my chief support in making this decision, although she also had very grave doubts about it. Having determined that this was what I wanted to do I went flat out for it. In fact I used to neglect my school studies in order to be able to practise.

I attended three schools and in the end did not take the leaving certificate. My parents tried all sorts of ways to try and make me attend to my studies. I was at one time at Sydney Grammar School, which has at various times been attended by all my brothers and now one of them, as I said before, is its headmaster. But this school was within walking distance of the conservatorium and it was all too easy for me to cut the games and even the odd class and go over to the conservatorium, either to practise the oboe or to hobnob with the students, who were all much older than me. Then, in order to make it more difficult for me to escape from school, I was sent to a boarding school: King's School, Parramatta. Special arrangements were made for me to go and study at the conservatorium, but it was then no longer possible to just walk across the road and the park to the conservatorium.

When I was quite young and still living in Vaucluse in the late 1920s or early 1930s my mother became a Catholic. My father didn't like this very much and it meant that the family was to some extent divided. An agreement, a sort of truce, was made between them that, regarding the education of the children, they would spend their early careers in Catholic schools and after that the boys would go to Sydney Grammar and the girls to a non-Catholic school on the North Shore line. So the five boys started off at St Aloysius' College in Milsons Point where we had our early training with the Jesuits.

This slight friction between our parents on the subject of religion, while it didn't dominate our lives, affected us to some extent. I never did become a Catholic and some of the other children embraced the church which some have left while others have remained. I'm not even sure which of them are which at the moment.

My mother had been immensely impressed by some books which her father had written, 'Post Mortem' and 'Mere Mortals'. He was a great intellectual and a great medical man, Dr Charles MacLaurin, and in his books he analysed great characters of history from a medical point of view. For instance, he pointed out that the reason that Henry VIII was so horrible was because he had certain diseases. He also had a nihilistic view of life: that there was no hereafter. He was an atheist and didn't believe that we were here for any other reason than just to live our lives as best we could. He was a typical agnostic liberal of the early part of the twentieth century, and I think that my mother was rather upset by her father's attitude to life and life after death. She adored him and was influenced by him, and yet somehow felt that this attitude towards life was wrong. After he died she started to take an interest in the Catholic Church and she spent a long time studying it before embracing it.

It made a great difference to our lives. In a way it has been a positive thing because although I've not become a Catholic I have a very good idea of what the Catholic point of view on matters is. I feel that I can appreciate the Catholic view of art, particularly musical art, and I'm very fond of baroque architecture and painting.

In 1947 when I went to England, I quickly realised that I wanted to be a conductor and not a composer and I went flat out to achieve that. The characteristics of a good conductor are the ability to project his will or his reading or feelings about the music to a whole lot of musicians who don't necessarily all feel the same about the music. Some of them are inspired; some of them are dedicated; some of them don't give a damn; they've all been brought up in different backgrounds and different styles of music and they must all be welded together and made to play as much as possible as one man. Extreme talent for music is not even necessary. It is better, of course, if you do have a great talent for music because then your ear can pick out small things that can be made better. But the job of the modern conductor has nothing to do with teaching the musicians to play, because even in the worst orchestra the musicians know how to play. The job of the conductor is to make them all play in one style, and the more he can inspire them to do that, the better is that conductor.

I was always fairly good at organising people, even as a child. I used to be always organising amateur performances and theatricals. I even once dared to do a puppet version of Wagner's *Siegfried* using the Wagner records we had for the sound. I had a set of books, now very famous and valuable, of the four Ring operas in English, illustrated by Arthur Rackham. I used to read these things over and over again, and I was immensely inspired by these extraordinary pictures. I was so impressed that when I first saw a Wagner opera performed in Covent Garden in 1947 and then later in Bayreuth, I was very disappointed that it didn't look like the Arthur Rackham pictures. But I really did know my Ring as well as anybody could with the music, the vocal scores, the pictures and the recordings that were available then.

As I look back over my life, there is very little I would change or do differently—a few details, perhaps, but conducting is the thing I'm good at and I think I'm the right man in the right job.

Phillip Adams

Phillip Adams is a partner in the advertising firm Monahan Dayman Adams, and in that capacity is the creator of the 'Life Be In It' advertising campaign, featuring the indolent Norm. But Adams' activities and interests stretch well beyond advertising.

He has produced the feature films Jack and Jill: a Postscript, The Naked Bunyip, The Adventures of Barry Mackenzie, Don's Party, The Getting of Wisdom *and the animated feature for adults,* Grendel.

Deeply committed to the renaissance of the Australian film industry, Adams was the foundation chairman of the Film, Radio and Television Board and of the Independent Feature Film Producers' Association. He was a foundation member of the Australia Council and has been Chairman of the Australian Film Institute. He also planned the structure of the South Australian Film Corporation for the Dunstan government.

Phillip Adams is well known through his newspaper columns which have appeared in The Australian, Nation Review *and* The National Times. *His column now appears regularly in the* Age, *the* Courier Mail, *the* Adelaide Advertiser *and* The Bulletin. *Collections of his columns have been published under the titles* Adams With Added Enzymes, The Unspeakable Adams *and* More Unspeakable Adams.

When I was a child, and thought as a child, I gazed up at grown-ups with a mixture of exasperation and determination. I was exasperated by their ineptitude with children, with their impatience at our problems and their inability to comprehend a three-foot-six-inch point of view. So I was determined to remember exactly what it felt like to be a kid, so that I might, one day, be a more successful parent.

Childhood was a totalitarian regime from which I was very glad to escape. Still, we sentimentalise that time, remembering it as so many sandcastles and party balloons. Too often we remember ourselves running through long grass in slow motion, with a dog at our side, like in those lyrical television commercials for cornflakes. Yet childhood was a time of indignities and injustice.

Phillip Adams

'Childhood is a foreign country. They do things differently there'. I look back on school with nothing but bitterness. I found it a time of monstrous boredom, when minutes seemed to stretch into weeks. My home life wasn't particularly good or successful either, and I always felt that we, grown-ups and kids, were just talking different languages to each other. The generation gap which has been well identified in recent times yawned just as widely then.

I spent the first couple of years of my life living in a Congregational manse in Maryborough, where my father was the local cleric, and my memories of that are very dim. I can remember seeing lightning for the first time as a child and, thinking the sky was on fire, rushing past the peppercorns into a dark study where my father was writing a sermon. That's about all I can remember of the first stage of my life, after which I went to live with a gnarled grandfather and rheumatic grandmother in what was then an outer suburb of Melbourne: East Kew.

My grandparents were, if you like, the local Steptoe and Son operation. They weren't into junk, they were into market gardening, growing chrysanthemums for Mother's Day and violets and stuff for the big market. But we lived in what was regarded as a disgrace to the neighbourhood—a rather battered old weatherboard surrounded by a burnt-looking pine hedge.

My father had gone charging off to the war as a padre. From memory he went off first of all in the airforce. Something terrible happened to him and he was removed from that branch of the armed services and returned as a 'chocko' with the army. During that time my mother had a romance with a very smooth and unpleasant businessman in the city. Having lived on a churchmouse income she was rather taken by this guy who drove a great big black Studebaker and who gave her the odd fur coat. She was very bitter about her life as a minister's wife, so when my father came back from the war the marriage immediately disintegrated. I lived right through the war years with my grandparents. I stayed with them until I was ten, when I moved in with my schizophrenic stepfather and mum in a flat in the city.

Living with my grandparents (they were my mother's parents) was quite a battle for a child. They were getting pretty old. Grandpa was a grumpy, remote old guy, but I realise in retrospect that he had enormous affection for me. He just didn't care to articulate it very much. He was brusque and distant—a bit like Soames Forsythe. But underneath it all he was a very warm old guy. And I had to look after my grandmother for a number of years when she was terribly ill. I remember as a kid of twelve lugging this very overweight old lady, crippled with rheumatism, down to the dunny, hauling off her knickers and putting her on the po. Then, shortly after that, my grandfather, who had always seemed to me as the Titanic sort of figure, an absolute Tree of Man, got rapidly, seriously ill. I watched him waste away with astonishment and disbelief. He just seemed to me to be immutable.

After grandpa's death, as I said, I moved in with mum and her new husband, who wasn't really the wealthy entrepreneur that she had imagined. He was a rather ordinary, failed businessman, who by then was reduced to being a book-keeper for a city engineering company. He was stark, raving mad, and from the age of twelve to sixteen I lived in a nightmare where I'd lie awake in bed waiting for him to start bashing my mother. I was living under such constant tyranny and tension that I developed all sorts of curious heart problems and various other psychosomatic ailments. He was quite authentically schizophrenic, I think, and these days would probably be certified, but one didn't do that sort of thing then. To the outside world he was all charm and decency; to my mother and me he was nothing but a sadist.

My father had returned to Melbourne after the war and for a while he was a chaplain or minister at various Congregational churches around the place. He was in terrible trouble with the Church. I suspect it was drinking problems or something—or just lack of theological commitment. He finished up reversing the Biblical parable about tax-gatherers in that he left the church and became one, working for the Taxation Department. I used to see him on the odd weekend, but many of those situations were fraught with tension. For example, probably the highlight and the most horrific day of my childhood, was when it was intended that I go down to see my father and meet his new wife. I heard from a third party that she looked like Yvonne de Carlo. I don't know if you remember her, but she used to wear a lot of harem trousers and mince around in films about Ali Baba. I was quite looking forward to meeting this beauteous creature. But before I, with my little, shabby suitcase, left to catch the train from Montmorency, there was a huge fight at the house. I remember knocking my stepfather over, to my astonishment. In fact I sent him flying across the room, pounding into the venetian blinds and leaving them buckled forever after. This was to defend my mother from physical attack. I remember then leaving in panic and fear and sort of belting down the long dusty road to the Montmorency station. He charged after me in his big, black car and tried to run me over. I only saved myself by hurling myself into the grass by the side of the road and hiding until he went away.

I got down to the Montmorency station, climbed on the train, and at the next station, which was Greensborough, there to my horror was this lunatic face in the window and his hand on the door. It was peak period and it seemed to me there were thousands of people milling around. He dragged me out of the carriage, threw my suitcase, scattered everything, screamed to everyone that I was a thief . . . it was the humiliation. I was used to the tantrums, but this was in public and I thought that everyone in the world was looking. Then he switched, with his usual skill, to being sweetly reasonable; apologised to the crowd, which was becoming a bit menacing with this display of his; got a bit tearful; said he was terribly sorry, that he would take me to my father in the car—because by now of course, the train was gone. I begged people not to put me in the car with him. I knew from bitter experience what was going to happen, but, you know, he seemed plausible and apologetic. Into the car I went, and I knew I was in for big, big trouble, so I flung myself out of the car as we drove past a police station.

I somehow got to see my father that night finally, and Yvonne de Carlo turned out to look more like the witch from the Wizard of Oz! I will never forget walking down the path to this little house he had and seeing this extraordinary woman trying to stab him with a pair of scissors. My father was screaming like a stuffed pig in terror, and, being a fairly ineffectual sort of character wasn't doing much to ward off the blows. As he ran out the door in horror I ran in and knocked her unconscious. That was when I first met my step-mother. My father and I then went out and sat in the car. I remember shaking, crying, you know, with the accumulated horrors of the day. I'll never forget what my great, big father said to me next. He said, 'Would you go into the house and get my wallet?'

So that was my childhood, I think, summed up. Living under great tension at home and not being able to rely on my natural father for support. So this taught me self-reliance and it taught me to be a survivor.

At school I was a very lonely, isolated kid. My scholastic performance was average. In retrospect it seems I spent most of my school years being sent to the headmaster and hiding in the dunny, or walking up and down the corridor with books under my arm looking like I was busy. I was obsessed with the size of my head, I remember. Rather cruelly, my middle name was Hedley. This had been given to me by my mother in the hope that my namesake, who was a businessman in Maryborough, would shower us with wealthy gifts. He never came through actually, so I was lumbered with this name, and I did have a rather large head. And, of course, with the name Hedley, and the feeling of being rather burdened with brains, I was often being sent up on that basis by other kids who saw me as a bit professorial, I guess. In every gang there's usually a Doc or a Prof. In so far as I got into other kids' gangs it was usually in that role. I really felt terribly strange and odd and like many people who have felt that sort of vulnerability (it goes for Barry Humphries, I know, and for people like Dudley Moore) you try to fight back with humour. I became the class clown as a method of ingratiating myself, protecting myself and getting some notice. So I did spend an awful lot of time in the corridor.

On the other hand I think my teachers were quite fond of me. It seems, in retrospect, as I meet one or two of them over the years, that they recognised I had a few problems, but thought I was better off in the corridor. So school years were a bit of a hell really. I didn't like sport. I felt my great balloon head was a huge obstacle in football, and although I was a strong and rather big kid for my age, I really was much happier sitting down in the quince orchards at Eltham High School trying to read books. But at most of the schools I attended this was deemed to suggest homosexuality, and so one was always thrust into sport. That meant you were lined up and the current school heroes would pick the teams, and I was always the last kid picked . . . or me and another boy called Johnny Straggler were always the shags on the rocks, the leftovers. I've always detested compulsory sport for that reason. I think that people forget that while it allows certain young men to soar high above their fellows, there are always the also-rans who are pilloried. So many a day I've spent tossing quoits in a woe-begone fashion, while the other heroes rushed around kicking their footies.

I read a lot as a child—the usual diet of Mary Grant Bruce (I don't know whether kids still read her in Australia); Biggles, who has rather faded from my memory; but best of all, during the early years, there were 'William' books by Richmal Crompton, which I still treasure more than Hemingway and Dos Passos. A couple of years ago I dared to go back to them to see whether they were as wonderful as I remembered, and they stand up very very well. They are very clever and very funny. Very anarchistic in lots of ways, with a very acute perception of the British class system and of pro-vincial village life. William, with his dog, Jumble, and his socks around his ankles and his dreadful mates and a little girl called Elizabeth who used to 'thcream and thcream till she was thick' when anything went wrong, just absolutely captivated me. I read like a maniac, as a result of loneliness, and I was also constantly writing as a survival technique.

I wrote, I guess, from the age of six, with a progressive manic energy to try and cope with what was happening, and in parallel I was reading. At the age of thirteen I had completely exhausted the kids' library at Kew and I went nervously to the librarian and asked for more. She was a very clever lady and gave me *The Grapes of Wrath* by Steinbeck, which then precipitated the falling-over of a whole series of intellectual dominoes. This led directly to my once and for all abandoning any religious attitudes I might have

111

had, and joining the Communist Party when I was sixteen or seventeen.

I wouldn't recommend my childhood to others. I think that many people who have had similar experiences have become very bitter. I guess I was lucky enough to have a very strong metabolism. I really think that's important and it's the luck of the draw. Leaving aside any questions of mental stability—that's a big help and I guess I had that—I was able to bounce back from really difficult situations. The problem wasn't so much the crises of the sort I could describe for hours, as the constant tension. The fact that I was always being abused, denigrated and bullied every minute of my life at home was the real horror. What I did to survive was to move into one room.

My house now is full of things stuck to the walls—there are faces from Egyptian sarcophagi, Roman portraits, Condor drawings, Bruce Petty's cartoons and all sorts of funny things around the room. What I did as a child was to smother the walls of my bedroom in our triple-fronted weatherboard with things I cut out of magazines. I've still got them all. I rescued them and they're all in a box in the garage. I looked through them a few months ago and they really were a very precocious collection. There were Ben Shahn drawings and all sorts of extraordinary things. I lived in that room, totally separated from what was going on in the rest of the house as a survival technique. I read and I wrote and fantasised. Fantasy of course is a wonderful method of coping, and my fantasies were fairly normal. I used to read the fairy stories of the industrial age— Superman, Captain Marvel, and, like most kids, I would identify with Robin in Batman comics or with Boy in the Tarzan films. I think many kids like me in fact sought for surrogate fathers in their comic books. One did tend to identify with these great big macho guys and they were very useful. But what really saved me was *The Grapes of Wrath*, because I suddenly realised that there was a world outside my own inevitably limited pre-occupations.

My isolation at that time was greatly intensified by my constant religious trauma. This had nothing whatsoever to do with my father being a minister. I have the most vague memories of that. But from about the age of six, I guess because I felt lost and alienated and in a sense alone in my little sleepout, I began to doubt the paternalism of the universe. I mean, that's a rationalisation now—it might have been much simpler than that. From the age of six I was constantly, consciously concerned with death. I don't mean being minced under a tram or falling off my bike, I'm not talking about *dying*; I'm talking about *non-existence*.

It's during the war. I'm living in my little sleepout, listening to Sankey's Sacred Songs on my crystal set (not that I liked them but they were the only thing I could get). The wind is soughing in the pine trees; the rain is falling on the galvo roof, surely the most exquisite sound in human experience. To me the war simply means an occasional aircraft caught on the flypaper of a searchlight. But I guess it added to my levels of anxiety. I'd pick up the signal from others. My father would occasionally appear on leave, sort of saffroned with malaria or whatever it was that soldiers got. Or an occasional coconut would turn up at the letter-box with 'Master Phillip Adams' hacked into its hide. And I'd lie in bed at night, five or six years old, and terrified by the thought of death.

I knew intuitively that the universe is completely senseless, meaningless—that there is no reason to it—that there's no paternal figure in the sky. I knew it, oddly enough, because of a curious sequence of logic. It occurred to me suddenly that infinite time and infinite space are the same thing. I make that fairly obvious connection. I find myself falling through the stars. I fall up through the roof of the sleepout, past the pine trees, up past the aeroplanes and the searchlight—falling outwards, which itself is an eerie experience. I'd fall for millions of miles through the stars and I'd say: 'This can't be! There has to be an ending. Things have a beginning, they have to have an ending'. I'm really dealing with the euphemism for eternity, and in my mounting terror I used to switch on the bedlamp, sit up in bed and say: 'My name is Phillip Adams of 798 High Street, East Kew', trying to ward off these absolutely apocalyptic terrors with a bit of meaningless data.

One night I found the experience of falling upwards so intolerable that I invented a rocky vault around the universe. It did have an ending. It had a huge rocky vault all the way around. I bounced off it with a great sense of relief, because that seemed to me to mean that time and space both had some sort of ending somewhere. But that only lasted a few months, because one terrible night I fell through the crust and instantly realised that it couldn't have an end, that just as surely as there always had to be a bit more space on the other side of any arbitrary rocky vault, there couldn't be an end to time. In that second I realised that the notion of God was irrelevant. Christianity seemed to me to have a most lopsided sort of diagram of existence. There had to be a creation, so you invent an original cause. But there can't be an end, so you postulate eternal life, and that seems to me to be the most unbalanced sort of see-saw.

Now a child of five or six then asks a very simple and a very reasonable question, which usually gets him a cuff across the ears, 'But who made God?' I know there are more sophisticated theological arguments these days, but to a child it's a fairly simple proposition. The argument went: there has to be a beginning, there has to be a creation and that is explained away by a God who can't have a beginning. So you don't really need the concept. Even at that stage I was vaguely willing, I suppose, to call everything God if you wanted to use that three letter word to embrace totality. But it did imply a consciousness, of course, and I just couldn't feel any sense of that at all.

Now atheists are like homosexuals, they don't come to this conclusion happily. Most homosexuals I know discover their sexual nature with a series of quite terrifying shocks, and I can assure you

that most atheists, in my experience, do not happily embrace that
black hole. They'd rather like there to be a father and a purpose
and a meaning and a destiny. Now, once that happened to me and
was subsequently compounded by my experiences with my stepfather and you add the two levels of dilemma together—a cosmic
alienation, which really dominated my life and always did until I
was eighteen or nineteen, and a sense of domestic alienation—
you're really in a pretty serious position. I survived simply by
thinking it out on paper, writing about it constantly, and also developing a fairly effective sense of the absurd. You don't really need
avant-garde philosophers to introduce the notion of the absurd
into the situation that I was in. Everything was ridiculous, and I
used to find that I could do a sort of helicopter shot, for instance,
when I was in the domestic situation with my stepfather or in any
sort of crisis: I'd just mentally take off, which I'm sure a lot of
people do. I'd just zoom up into the sky and it's like the thing you
write in your exercise book when you're a kid: 'Phillip Adams,
High Street, East Kew, Melbourne, Victoria, Australia, the Southern
Hemisphere, the World, the Universe'. You do that sort of micro-
cosm-macrocosm zoom-out and suddenly you realise that you're
just not important. Hence the appropriateness to me of Steinbeck,
who tried to put this traumatised, neurotic child into a social
awareness of other people's problems. I leapt on it as a surrogate
religion. So it was inevitable that I'd be a communist, for however
brief a term—and it was inevitable also that I'd find my co-religion-
ists (because communism is certainly a religion as much as Catholicism) tended to share exactly these sorts of backgrounds.

The happiest moments of my childhood were times spent with
my dog. I had a beaut, wobbly, funny bitzer of a dog. I have happy
memories of swimming in the dam with her. And I loved climbing
trees and I rejoiced in going to the matinees at Hoyts.

I think that, to some extent, I am a better parent because I do
remember my own childhood. When I first married I'm afraid I

was so polluted by my stepfather's tyranny that I tended to react to it. I think this is a fairly common phenomenon. You know, the sins of the stepfathers are visited on the sons, and for a while I found myself just as much a bully and just as much an authoritarian thug as he had been. I needed quite a bit of healing, which my young wife managed to provide, bless her heart. Then I remembered my pledge made as a child and I tried to be a good parent. The reality is that it is a bloody big chore and if you're super-busy and the sort of hyperactive lunatic I am, being a good parent is rather more than a full-time job. You tend to fall back on the same cliches with your children that your parents used on you. There will be a fracas between a couple of kids and you won't really bother to adjudicate, to play the Solomon, you will arbitrarily agree with one of them, and you know you're being unjust. But it's efficient and it will get you out of the situation. I also find it's often quite useful to be a bit thick as a parent, to not really get the signals that the kid is getting from you, because that involves sitting down and talking to them for an hour and you mightn't have an hour. So I think I've finished up being a better parent than I would have been had I not had those experiences, but I'm far from an ideal parent and I generally feel a lot of guilt about it.

My talent is for survival and, because I had to articulate my own dilemma, I tend to think fairly freely and, I think, accurately about the nature of relationships. I write now, as I wrote then, as a form of therapy.

I'd much rather be a prime minister or a brain surgeon or an ambassador to Paraguay or some such thing, but when I was fifteen I had no hope of getting to university—I didn't even matriculate. I had to get out of my terrible home-life and a couple of teacher friends at Eltham High got me a part-time holiday job working in an advertising agency for an extraordinarily gifted and a deeply cultured man called Haughton James. He, in fact, started some of the great art magazines in Australia during the 1950s, and was a very erudite, scholarly and eccentric fellow. They paid me £5 a week for riding a push-bike down to the trade houses picking up flong and stereos. This meant that I could leave home, so I did. I was then to find that advertising fulfilled a very useful social function for people like myself. It's fascinating to look at the novelists, painters, cartoonists and musicians, all of them prominent in Australia now, who all worked in advertising in pre-Australia Council days. It was the only sort of renaissance prince around that would pay people of vague and anarchistic talents a quid, and I've been in it ever since. Obviously I use it as some sort of power base for other activities. It gives me a lot of freedom in many ways to do other things.

All of the childhood experience paid off, in a way. The fact that I wrote obsessively meant that I was fluent and I could write very well for most purposes. My obsession with death gave me an unusual insight and I was able to take a position as writer that was not all that common. So after a while I've been able to look back on my childhood with nothing short of profound gratitude. I'm now bloody glad that I had such a hideous childhood. Had I not had it I'm sure I would have just sunk into oblivion in some way.

Thomas Keneally

Thomas Keneally is one of Australia's best known authors with a considerable output of novels and plays to his credit. His first novel, The Place At Whitton, was published in 1964 and his second, The Fear, in 1965. He says: 'I cringe every time I think of my first two novels. They misdirected whatever talent I have. But my third, Bring Larks and Heroes, is a good novel. I know it is and I hope I can say so without sounding conceited.' Bring Larks and Heroes was produced on a Commonwealth Literary Fund grant and for it he won the Miles Franklin Award in 1967. He was then able to write full-time.

In 1969 he won equal first prize in the Cook Bi-Centenary Novel award with The Survivor. Keneally claims that his favourite work is the bizarre novel A Dutiful Daughter (published in 1971) in which a young woman has to cope with the metamorphosis of her parents into cattle.

Keneally has had three plays produced and has himself become a film actor in Fred Schepisi's two feature films, The Devil's Playground and The Chant of Jimmie Blacksmith, the film of his own novel of 1972.

At seventeen Thomas Keneally went straight from school into the seminary to train for the priesthood but he decided just before he was to be ordained that he was mistaken in his calling. His early novel Three Cheers For The Paraclete gives an insight into his attitude to the priesthood in the 1960s.

In 1979 his latest novel Passenger was published.

I was born in Sydney on 7 October 1935 and my earliest memory is of when we were living in Kempsey, I sat backwards into a basin of boiling water.

The most significant memory I have of my early childhood is of being an only child—at least until the time I was eight. I also remember the experience of getting diphtheria or some severe respiratory illness that was diagnosed as diphtheria. That happened on the day I started school, when I was five, and I have written something of the delirium into a children's novel which is about to be published. I can also remember odd things like playing in a dress shop which belonged to my aunts and father, playing with a cousin, often with boiled lollies in our mouths and hands and playing among the dress racks, giving everyone concern about what we were going to do to the fabrics. But the most enduring memory I have of that time is of the political continuity. Even at that stage I was aware of being separate from the Anglo-Saxon Australians, a feeling that was very strong in both my father's family and my mother's.

I had a strong sense of being Irish and of being Catholic. We had different politics—Labor Party. We had this sense of not having had a fair go in the Depression. I didn't even know there was such a thing as the Depression, but I'm sure that it sparked a lot of that sort of talk. We had a sense of not having the sort of loyalties that other people in the community had, like loyalty to Britain and the Empire and the Royal Family. I can certainly remember all that and I think that has coloured the political ideas that I've got now, vaguely republican and vaguely Labor Party.

I hope I'm not mythologising the whole thing, but I think there was a strong feeling that Australia was potentially a Utopian country. This idea was encouraged by our isolation, and Australia was seen as a white sheet on which a new history could be written. It promised the possibility of escaping the pernicious influences of the northern hemisphere. It was specifically a family like mine that felt a certain separation from the normal Britannic aspirations of other groups. Disappointment at the failure of the Utopian dream was most acute.

I remember the early years of the war fairly coherently. I remember the absence of the men; the Americans being here; the *Queen Mary* coming through the heads with the troops from the Middle East. I was brought home from school the day the Japanese reconnaissance planes flew over Sydney. I can remember the night, almost like Thurber's *Night The Ghost Got In*, when the Japanese submarines came into Sydney Harbour. I can remember very acutely, as just about every Australian who grew up then can, that sense of being a small but somehow destinied race— a sense that people had more strongly then than now, that people like Curtin personified.

My father is a very good raconteur with a very good grasp of that rich Australian argot of rhyming slang and the earthy bush imagery that older Australians still have. I think if there is any wit in what I have written I got it from him. He was the youngest of nine children and experienced some period of unemployment in the Depression. He was also a local town football hero in the first-grade Rugby League team in Kempsey and Taree. But there was a great melancholy about him as well as being a gnomic, vivacious person in company. This great streak of melancholy expressed itself in dissatisfaction with himself and with his destiny and with the state of the world.

Even as a child I can remember him expressing dissatisfaction with himself and lack of confidence in himself in various ways. I can also remember heavy depressions. He came from a family that was spectacularly manic, and while he never had any alcohol problems there were some in the family who did. There was also a marked eccentricity combined with this extraordinary melancholy. He combined vivacity with sadness which is a characteristic Australian contradiction. He is a conservative radical, a bush lawyer and a wild melancholic. There was always in his family a self-restlessness of spirit and self-dissatisfaction. It was that Wandering Jew sort of temperament which I have myself to an extent. I find life is a little bit like sliding down a cliff face and you wouldn't want it any other way, but you are plagued by restlessness in connection with the work you're doing now and what might happen in the future and so on.

My mother's family had the same characteristics. Her father and grandfather were restless Irishmen. Her grandfather had lived in Ireland, Australia and America and had moved back and forth following the gold veins in the 1850s. He had even been in the American army.

My mother was not nearly as eccentric as my father's family. She was a characteristic country girl of her era, in that she had an acute desire for education and yet she had to leave school in sixth grade. Perhaps as a consequence the biggest issue in my childhood was education. They made sure my brother and I went to the best school available.

We went to Christian Brothers', Strathfield, which was considered to be much better than Christian Brothers', Burwood, because it had a fifth year. The fees at Strathfield were quite expensive, because it was a school for the lower middle classes. It existed to turn the kids who went there into surgeons and engineers and, like most Christian Brothers' schools in the 1930s and 1940s, it succeeded incredibly in producing this sort of metamorphosis. In a strange sort of way, therefore, it was an extremely materialistic, success-oriented school, in which all the staff were Irish and Australian brothers living with oaths of poverty and quite simple and deprived lives and yet geared to this idea of turning everyone—except those who became priests or brothers—into surgeons and engineers and so on.

I remember my parents' devotion to book learning as something that they had been deprived of and that they wanted their children to get at any cost. They had a respect for books that I think was universal in Australia at that time. It was considered a good thing to read and an honourable thing to write and there was a stress on education as a means of survival. That was an idea that had grown out of the Depression, too, and a lot of families had it. I'm reminded of Mordecai Richler, the Canadian writer, who quotes his grandmother in one of his books: 'So what do those Protestants care if their kids don't grow up to be brain surgeons . . .' and that was pretty well the atmosphere in our family.

We were always fairly hard up. We didn't have a car. Our parents didn't go out much in those days. There was great concentration on things like school uniforms and school shoes. It seemed to my brother and me that a great part of the income went on school expenses, and I'm sure that it did. Our parents wouldn't have made us deliberately aware of that, but it was impossible not to be aware of it, because funds were short. There was no State help in those days and it was a great struggle for them.

I was a very slow and ill co-ordinated child and I was the dunce of the class till I was about twelve. This was extremely painful. I had two burning ambitions—one was to be a good footballer, and I was so ill co-ordinated as a small child that I couldn't quite manage it. I was plagued with respiratory troubles and asthma and I had innumerable pneumonias as a child. I seemed to pick up infections extremely easily, but I had the normal sporting ambitions that all Australian children have. I think sport is very important in the Australian mentality. I think Manning Clark at one level of his being probably considers himself a failed ruckman who was forced to write history brilliantly to compensate for not having played for Carlton. I think there are a lot of Australians like that.

I was so mentally and physically ill co-ordinated as a child, and missed so much early schooling through illness, that I couldn't fulfil either my sporting or my academic ambitions until round about the age of puberty, or a year or so before, when everything fell into place. I could suddenly do the things that I'd never done before. I don't mean the normal things that boys start doing at puberty, I mean maths and geometry. Then I had a very happy high school career and became better co-ordinated. I started to run for the school and to get into a few football teams. I started to develop literary ambitions fairly early, but only in the vague way that kids have who want to play for the Australian Rugby League team or want to be in the movies. I had this ambition only in the vaguest sense, but it expressed itself in a fairly literary cast of mind and in a tendency to write little memoirs and start novels.

I can remember that my father was at that stage working away from home on the railways and he brought home one of those cricket matches made out of two dies which you throw across the floor and one die has the score from 1 to 6 on it and the other one has the various ways you can get out. I used to play that by the hour with two teams, one a team of composers and the other a team of writers. I used to have immense fun looking up an old *Cassell's Encyclopedia* that we had and picking the writers' team and picking who'd be twelfth man. It was quite a mental thrill to be able to make Mendelssohn twelfth man!

I received considerable encouragement in my literary interests. I was encouraged to read, but of course in those days it was considered a preposterous thing for an Australian to write a book. I mean, I'd never heard of an Australian writing a book. I didn't think you could.

I must attack the sort of curriculum we had in those days. Even when I got into high school in 1948 we had a curriculum which I am quite convinced was aimed at turning us into loyal sons of the Empire. We studied no Australian literature, except in the junior high school when we might have read 'The Man From Snowy River' and 'The Bellbirds'. We studied mainly romantic poets up to Tennyson and I got the feeling that Australia was outside the literary hemisphere and that it was impossible to have literary ideas about Australia. One of the things that broke this down was a Christian Brother who was a very contradictory man. He was a great man, I might say: a fine opening batsman, and very sensitive. He used to play records to the kids whom he used to select to get into his unofficial music appreciation class, which was a matter of great *éclat* for the chosen. He introduced me to Hopkins and Greene and T. S. Eliot. At the same time he was telling us that women aren't interested in sex and everyone must realise this and make allowances for it. While misleading us in that way he was introducing us to this extraordinary range of modern writing, including things like Somerset Maugham's *Cakes and Ale* which contradicted, of course, everything that he was telling us about women and sexuality. So I remember him as being a crucial person. His impact on me was one of the things that led me into studying for the priesthood.

I can remember discovering the modern poets and carrying around in the pocket of my school uniform the Brother's *Albatross Book of Modern Verse*. I was so excited by it that I wanted to change cells with it somehow. It became dog-eared and I had to buy him a new copy for his little library. Then after I'd wrecked one edition of the *Albatross Book of Modern Verse* I wrecked an edition of Gerard Manley Hopkins on him. So by the time I was in fourth year I was starting to get very literary indeed, but I still wanted to be in the school football team.

It was in early 1952 that I decided that I wanted to be a priest. As anyone who's seen Ron Blair's *The Christian Brother* knows there are considerable urgings in that direction for anyone who felt he had the call—the Vocation. In those days the priest, historically, had a strange but not unexciting position in the community. He had considerable political power. He was still in the tradition of the Irish peasant and a leader of his people. He was still the cleverest man—or, *considered* to be the cleverest man in the parish. I think I was attracted by the intellectual side of it—all that scholastic philosophy and theology. The other thing was that I felt, as a

125

great number of us did, sexually uncertain, particularly uncertain about the marriages that we saw in our daily life. The average Irish Catholic marriage didn't look like the greatest thing on wheels to an adolescent. In those days you didn't have recourse to the alternatives that you do today: no one cleared out to Bali or went to the Barrier Reef and became a beach bum. And in a way becoming a priest was an attractive proposition. I don't want to run the priesthood down, or myself, because I think it was a decision made in good faith and I think a lot of kids made it in good faith, but I think one of the attractions was this idea that you had power over your community and power, particularly, over women. You had that power and yet didn't have to put up with the abrasion of living with anyone. In those days being a priest was a far more political thing than it is now, because of the long association of the Catholic clergy with the Labor Party, which was only just ending when I was a child. The whole Evatt, Petrov, Santamaria thing was just coming to a head.

My mother and father were fairly bemused by the Split. They didn't vote according to the Church line, but they were aggrieved at Evatt and they tended to be very confused by it. My mother stayed with the Labor Party, but it wasn't the same party it had been. Curtin and Chifley were sort of saints and they both came from the same Irish Catholic tradition and they both had that specialness and destiny which struck a chord with my parents. They saw Evatt as an opportunist and a sectarian, because that's what the papers and the *Catholic Weekly* told them to see him as. I can remember that at school the Brothers' community was split down the middle, some of them sticking with the New South Wales Joe Cahill sort of Labor politics and others going to the DLP—and the latter, particularly, proselytising in the classroom.

The Catholic faith was, and still is, very important to my parents. Attendance at Mass and so on are extremely important. If they were Jewish people I suppose you'd call them 'moderate Orthodox'.

I think as well as getting some comfort from it they felt a bit bound to it and dominated by it, because it was a very dominating sect in those days.

My father went to the war in 1942 and served in the Middle East, Palestine, Egypt and Libya. He came home in late 1945 and I remember those post-war years as being extremely drab, plagued by strikes. The city seemed to be full of bewildered Europeans. There seemed to be a lot of cooking in backyards in those late 1940s during the coal strikes and power strikes. There was a disenchantment among the adults who felt that when the war ended there'd be a golden time, and of course there wasn't, and some of that disenchantment rubbed off on me. As early as that I was aware of Australia having no history and no dimension to it, and being discontented with that.

My mother was the dominant parent in my childhood, which I think is a temperamental thing. I think she's the stronger of the two and also we were on our own for three years. My brother was born about three or four months after my father left with the army and we were very aware of forming a sort of *laager*, an embattled camp. During those years alone my mother would have been the dominant influence, but she would have been anyway, because as I said she was the stronger of the two. She was less markedly a victim of the terrible spiritual restlessness.

My father is very dominant in my thinking and I've often thought of writing a novel about him, or his type of Australian. He's now seventy and would have been young in the 1920s when the Depression hit and I think that shook up the Australian jaunty self-confidence. It was also the beginning of the drift to the cities and they became the bushmen in the cities, dislocated, expatriated country boys. Then the relief from the Depression was World War 2 and since 1950 they've been in the city wondering what it all meant and where it all went to. I think Australians like him have very much that sense of specialness and the possibility of Utopia.

My maternal grandfather was a strong influence on me. He was himself tiny, physically very strong and had worked everywhere. His patron saint would have been John Curtin, and he saw society as a Masonic plot. But in spite of that influence and the influence of the school I was not conscious of any anti-Protestant hostility. Our attitude to Protestants was one of pity. We called other people 'non-Catholics' which implied a sort of failure on their part. It wasn't intellectual tolerance, that wasn't taught from the pulpit or the rostrum in the school; it was pity. You were taught by the Brothers to pity the poor kids who were taught by teachers who were married and have concerns other than their teaching. You were taught that Protestants can only go to heaven if they are afflicted with something called 'Invincible Ignorance'. So generally Protestantism was looked on as a terminal disease which a lot of people had through no fault of their own. The atmosphere at Christian Brothers' was of being in a camp that was going to win. We were like the slight underdogs in the premiership who had all the right moves. It was an extremely confident attitude, but there was prejudice. We were told what public service departments were controlled by the Knights of the Southern Cross, and therefore which departments to get into.

There was also a dichotomy in the consciousness with which we studied our subjects. Roberts' *History of Modern Europe*, for example, which we studied in New South Wales, was an extremely Britannic and Masonic view of history, but we were taught it because that was the one that would get us through the exam. As the Christian Brother in Ron Blair's play says, we were taught not to put anything on the paper that would give away our sectarian origins. We were not to call the Pope 'the Holy Father', for instance, and we had to pretend to be delighted with what Cavour did to the Papal States, and to pretend that we were delighted about the French Revolution. So there was a split consciousness.

I have two children of my own—two girls. In bringing them up

I've tried to make sure that they are exposed to books. Although they don't know it they've been systematically exposed to books from an extremely early age, and because I've worked at home so much I've been able to read to them. Until they could read for themselves they used to get the better part of an hour at night reading, because I had this intuitive conviction that kids who get read to end up reading themselves. Besides this they also get very articulate, and a lot of educationalists have said that this is true. I also used to read to them because of the thrill of seeing them apprehend things, and no one enjoys a book like a child. In Fiji I read my daughters *The Hound of the Baskervilles*. They could read it themselves, but I did it so I could witness the excitement of the first contact with something like Sherlock Holmes.

Although Catholicism has become more benign, in a way, I was sure that my children shouldn't be educated as Catholics. You know, I doubt that benignity. I think that the last two Popes have shown that there is a hard, impermeable core to the whole thing.

A member of the State Parliament, who has had the same upbringing as me, and no longer practises 'The Faith', as it's called, said that it's a bit of a shock to think that you're the first member of your family since the Dark Ages who hasn't been a Catholic. It's a bit awesome. You wonder if you are doing the dirt on all the others. But when we were young there was that political cause and tribal reason for being a Catholic. Now it's entirely different. We've got bishops accepting knighthoods and they all vote Liberal. You've just got to say 'condom' and they think that Asiatic atheistic communism is just round the corner. There isn't even the tribal political cause to make it valid that the kids should get that sort of education.

My children have made their first Communion at their own insistence and they go to Catholic Scripture, by their own choice, at the State school. On the subject of religion I've communicated certain things to them, things like the fact that I don't think there is any sense in telling your crimes to another man, because I don't think people know what their crimes are. If Hitler had gone to confession he would have confessed to swearing at Eva Braun; he wouldn't have had any insight into his true sins. I have also taught them that I think stupidity is one of the worst evils that accounts for half the world's grief. But I also can't conceal from them that I have always had the temperament and tendency to the mystical—a sort of apprehension of 'The Other', or whatever you want to call it. I still believe in 'The Other' or 'The Absolute'. I still believe in that as naturally as believing in anything, even though it's unprovable. I suppose my children have taken from me a certain sense of the metaphysical absolute, although they wouldn't call it that.

By the time that my children had got to an age where we could talk about these things I had become entirely dissociated from the Catholicism that rated so highly in my childhood. What had happened was that first I left the seminary shortly before ordination and I clung to that old 1950s Catholicism for a very short period before I started to become a radical ratbag. Then the next phase was trying to make Catholicism into something more liberal, trying to exploit Vatican Two and mixing with trendy young blokes I'd known in seminary who were saying family Eucharists and speaking at anti-Vietnam demonstrations. They were suddenly extremely politically activated and were getting a heady thrill from shocking their bishops. They were getting the excitement of doing things priests had never done before and were coming to terms with their celibacy in ways that didn't take literal account of the Canon law. I can remember being on a committee of protest about the pill. Then the next phase, as these people were knocked off one by one, was thinking that all this was not worth exercising yourself about. All that theological controversy over the pill began to seem to me to be an irrelevance and I found I really didn't care. I cared so little that the idea of not bringing up my kids as Catholics wasn't a passionate idea. It wasn't a matter of kneeling at the altar of humanism and saying that I will not raise my children as Catholics. It was just that the thing had come to mean so little in its conventional form that it just happened.

Reflecting on my own childhood, I think that I could have been a little cosseted and I have attempted not to cosset my two. But that I would say is my greatest difficulty as a parent—I find it hard not to be an attentive parent, even at times when attention might not be welcome. But I've tried to give them a very strong physical dimension to their life, with things like sport and horse-riding. I think that adds grace to life. I'd hate them to become sports-women, but I don't tell them that and they will if they want to.

Another thing I've tried to do for my children is expose them to the natural environment. I expose them to animals, like the possums who live in our trees for instance, even at the risk of being pecked and scratched.

I also try not to have expectations about them. In my parents' generation I think it was necessary for them to have expectations for my brother and me. I don't think that's necessary anymore. I'm not even sure that these girls will be employed. So I never create expectations except that they won't go in beauty contests and that they won't be someone's Girl Friday!

The Chant of Jimmie Blacksmith

Fred Schepisi

Fred Schepisi, one of Australia's foremost film-makers, was born on 26 December 1939.

After leaving school at fifteen years of age he had a number of jobs until in 1960 he took charge of television commercial production for a major Melbourne advertising agency. In 1964, at the age of twenty-five, he joined Cinesound Productions, Victoria, as manager. Two years later he took the company over and founded Film House Pty Ltd. As managing director of Film House, Schepisi has written, produced and directed cinema and television documentaries, sales and public relations films and commercials.

His first venture in feature film-making was 'The Priest', a one half-hour segment of the film Libido.

His first full-length feature film, The Devil's Playground, tells the story of a young boy's experiences in a Roman Catholic junior seminary and, as Schepisi himself acknowledges, was based on his own childhood recollections. He wrote, produced and directed this highly successful film, which in the year of its release won almost all of the annual Australia Film Institute Awards, including those for Best Picture and Best Actor.

His second feature film, The Chant of Jimmie Blacksmith, based on the novel of Thomas Keneally, was Australia's most ambitious and expensive film project at the time of its production in 1977. This film had the honour in 1978 of being the first Australian film accepted as an official entry in the open competition in Cannes Film Festival. The film did disappointing business in Australia on its first release, but was well-received overseas, particularly in the U.K. where it was given critical acclaim. Schepisi says here that he was reconciled to losing his $200,000 investment in the film, but at the time of writing it appears that income from the British release of the film will return all of his outlay.

There was a great deal of my own childhood in *The Devil's Playground*. In fact it was about 70 per cent autobiography, combining events from my life in an ordinary boarding college which I had attended—Assumption College in Kilmore—and the strange environment and events of the Marist Brothers Juniorate at Macedon. But it was all quite tempered down. I felt that if I showed it as it actually happened ordinary audiences would never believe it. I thought they'd say: 'Oh, God, does it go that far?' So I pulled back a bit so that they could believe in it. Now I think it's probably a little bit too laid-back. I started writing it five years before it was first shown and there had been an enormous change in our acceptance of things in that time. Now I could probably push it a bit further. When I started writing it the only time you saw any frontal nudity was at the film festival, and even that caused a furore, so something as simple as two boys feeling one another, even among all the brambles, I felt would cause a shock. Five years took a lot of that reaction away, I think.

The Devil's Playground was not an unsympathetic or hostile film, you know. To me those Brothers were men who believed they were doing the right thing, but they themselves were struggling within that institutionalisation. They'd come up through the same system themselves and had missed out on great sections of life. But they were doing their work with an honest approach. Some of them were a little strange or peculiar because they *had* come up that way . . . But one of the things I wanted to say in the film is that in any group of people you will find a full spectrum of personalities.

Much of the dialogue for the film I could reproduce from memory of conversations I had overheard in the Kilmore college. I was in the infirmary a few times, one section of which was on the balcony outside the window of the Brothers' billiard room, and I could hear snippets of conversation and the sounds of the boozing and the game playing. Then, when I went to Macedon to the Marist

Brothers I always stayed back a few days at the end of term for some reason. Originally the boys were never allowed home for holidays, but not long after I'd come there they started allowing kids to go home for holidays, but for some reason which I can't remember, I always hung around for four or five days. I'd volunteer to stay back and help clean up. Well, then you get quite intimately involved in the Brothers' night life. They tended to relax and drink and try to show you that they were really human beings when they were on holidays. Some of those experiences came out in the film.

I had just turned thirteen when I entered the Marist Brothers' Juniorate, and at that stage I intended to become a Brother. But I only stayed there for eighteen months. It had been entirely my decision to go to Macedon. I don't think my parents were terribly enamoured of the idea. I think they believed that the best way, when confronted with anything like that, was to allow it to happen. I don't think they thought I'd go through with it, so rather than prevent me doing it and making a big issue out of it for the rest of my life, they allowed me to find out for myself what it was like.

I'd been at a boarding school, Assumption College, Kilmore, from the age of eight because I'd had a tubercular condition as a kid and I had to go up to the country. In those days it was believed that you had to be in the country to get the clean air and rest, I guess. At the school I got to know and like a few of the Brothers. And at these schools you're constantly being talked to, both *en masse*, as a school, and in individual counselling, to see if you have a 'Vocation'. We had visiting Redemptorist and Carmelite priests and a couple of them always seemed to take a shine to me. I would get out of class and have some free time talking to this guy who cracks jokes and you get to like him. I think they sense that they can work on you a bit and they sow the seed and you build on it yourself. Then one night you're sitting there with all the glory of benediction going on around you, and smooth satin robes and incense everywhere, and you think, 'Gee, this wouldn't be bad!' It's a very emotional decision. At twelve it's strictly the result of influence.

My parents were never devout Catholics, though my father is Australian-born of Italian parents and my mother of Irish. My father's father, who came out from Italy, also married an Irish lady. My parents chose my boarding school at Kilmore mainly because it had a quite high scholastic standard and they could afford it. My elder brother was stuck there with me, too, and I don't think he's ever forgiven me!

I didn't like boarding school very much at all. I didn't see much of my parents—they would come up every two or three weeks. The school was far too rigid and cold and there was really no love involved. I wouldn't send any of my kids to a boarding school.

I used to wet the bed and that's not a particularly exciting way to live. If you're at all peculiar or out of the run of the mill at a boarding college then you become the object of a hell of a lot of attention. The other kids get rid of their frustrations on you. It's quite a cruel environment. It wasn't a particularly good school—although there were a lot of aspects that I enjoyed and I'm sure that it's done something for me and has helped me to be independent—but I also know that it made me a very rigid person in my thinking. I used to see everything in black and white, and based on religion. It was a long time before I could think of anything clearly, and it made me very emotionally unstable for years. In fact even when you start to break out of that mould you don't realise how much it still influences the way you behave. Now, I'm sure some people would really survive and enjoy boarding school, but I don't think I did.

I don't blame my parents at all, in any way. They believed they were doing the right thing and that it was toughening me up. People really thought like that in those days, and after my junior years I handled it fairly well. But I will never forget when we used to have something called a 'bushie', where the leaders would select their ten best friends and all go out for a 'bushie'. All the peculiar guys—there were about seven of us—were always left over standing under the stairs. When everybody had picked their groups there were always some groups which were short and we would be allocated to a group of people who didn't want us. Those things stay with you for a long time.

I coped with this problem by being an idiot generally. Not as much as I've heard Dudley Moore say, not to that extent—but I used to do daring things. I'd jump off high river banks into very shallow water, or dive in among the bulrushes. God knows why I didn't cripple myself. I suppose they were just attention-getting actions, but I never thought of them like that at all. Apart from that, basically I just hung around with the stranger group of people and would occasionally fit in with the groups.

So from the age of eight to the age of fourteen I was in boarding school. I left Macedon when I was fourteen and went to Marcellin, a very soft college, for the last six months. I didn't want to go on scholastically any more—I'd finished, I wasn't interested in school after that.

I have retained none of my religious beliefs or interests. I think religion is an absolute farce. I think religion has a lot to answer for down the ages, and has caused more suffering and more problems for people than should ever have been possible. I went to Lebanon just before they had the war and had the opportunity to go to a place called Baalbek and also a place called Byblos. Byblos is where the Phoenician civilisation was, and there you can see city upon city that was built because of either wars or earthquakes. Standing above it all is a castle built by the Crusaders. Over this early civilisation comes imposed this religion, in the most strategic position possible. At Baalbek is one of the largest Roman ruins left. You walk into this place and see the Christian ikons with their heads knocked off—the Turks did that in the name of another religion. Then another came and got rid of all the Turks' pagan things and put their own objects in and so on. In this one place you can see how every few years some new religion or institution came in trying to force itself on the community. I think it's a great example of what's wrong with religion.

My disillusionment with religion came over a long time, but finally, when in my twenties I found myself yelling out at sermons in Mass, I figured it was time I stopped going. But the conditioning you have had since you were a baby is very hard to get rid of. I'm nearly thirty-nine now and sometimes I think I'm making rational decisions and suddenly I'll pull myself up and realise that that's something that is still part of my conditioning. I hadn't gone through any rational thought to arrive at the answer I'd just given. I actually blame organised religion for a lot of the things I feel about God, you know. If he exists I think he's a bit of a dill.

My mother was a very kind, gentle person. She used to talk to us a lot and fill us in on all the homey gossip and she would always make sure that we ate well and got most of the things that we needed. My father, on the other hand, was from a much sterner family. While he took us around a lot and played a lot of games with us, he was very strict. He believed that we should be brought up to fend for ourselves and his whole attitude was that we should be made independent as early as we possibly could, because that's how we were going to have to face life.

He used to play the odd joke by asking us to jump out of things into his arms and practically dropping us to teach us never to trust anybody. He'd occasionally cheat at cards and tell us later and could never quite understand why I'd say: 'Yeah, but I don't expect *you* to cheat! I get the point, but I don't expect *you* to cheat, you know.' He just said: 'Don't trust anybody!' Which was part his joke and part the truth. He also encouraged independence by giving us very definite duties and very definite disciplines that

138

we had to perform and by trying to get us to think for ourselves. I think that his concentration was a little too business oriented in getting on with the world and making money. But I think in both his and my mother's case their whole aim in life was to give us a better advantage than they had, which is fair enough. My father has been very successful in business. He started with a fruit shop and then was one of the first people into used cars, which he started in the back of the fruit shop. Then he changed into commercial vehicles, used trucks and so on, and now he's into land development.

Probably because of the way I've been brought up and hereditary influences, making money plays quite an important part in my life, because if I don't make it and I haven't got it then I can't do the things that I want to do. But having striven for it and made it I don't care if I then lose it doing the thing that I want to do. For instance I have $200,000 in *The Chant of Jimmie Blacksmith* and when I put it in I was quite prepared to lose it, as in fact I have. I don't think you ever make money unless you take the ultimate chance each time. So on the one hand I'm pulled and driven but on the other I don't really care. Sometimes I wish that I was a little freer, but life sort of gets you trapped into commitments with your various families, and you can't really change that.

My brother and I are quite different, you know. He's more conventionally logical and mathematical than I am. The best way to describe the difference is to tell about a game we played. We were going to fly troops from Melbourne to Sydney and he would lift up his aeroplane and he would fly it through the air for the obligatory six seconds and put it down again. I'd pick up my plane and put it in Sydney! He'd say: 'You can't do that! Sydney's 600 miles away ... ' and he'd go on about how many miles an hour you can fly so that it would take so long to get there. I said: 'Bullshit! That's Sydney and that's where I'm going'. Which I think illustrates the basic difference between us.

Apart from my parents there were some other adults who had an influence on me. There was one Brother in particular who was a genuine zealot as a teacher. He was an extraordinary man. I don't think anyone in his class has ever failed his subjects, which ranged from English through Geography to Latin. His name was Brother Osmond, and he managed to imbue his pupils with considerable enthusiasm which caught everybody up, and I think that's a remarkable talent.

I started work at an advertising agency when I was fifteen as a despatch boy. I pointed out to them that the three boys they had in despatch plus the guy who was in charge seemed to be rather a waste of time when they could have a car and driver do our work in one-fifth the time and also be able to ferry people around. So that buggered that job, but fortunately I was moved into another department where I did press productions. I'm not being egotistic, but I was quick on picking up the stuff, and my interest didn't hold that long. I reorganised the filing and then I'd say, 'Please give me that brochure to typeset'. They'd say, 'Go away kid! You're too fast!' Fortunately a couple of times people got sick and I got to do it all. So I'd done that, and I used to drive the manager mad. At sixteen I wanted to be an account executive. Then television came and they were able to get me into this new area. It gave me a fantastic opportunity because nobody in the film companies knew all that much. I could write things and then go down to the film company and put it into practice. I'd learn it along with them.

At this time I became fascinated with continental movies, because they had sex in them. I can remember stealing into *One Summer of Happiness* and thinking: 'I'm going to be excommunicated, but I don't care!' However having gone in I couldn't work out what the fuss was about. I mean, this lady lay on her back and her tits disappeared!I think this was the biggest disappointment I'd ever come across, but I found myself enjoying the film. Phillip

Adams got me hooked onto going to film societies and then festivals and my interest grew from there, almost by accident.

I knew then that I had to get out of advertising into film, so I put my age up a few years and got the job of manager of Cinesound in Melbourne which had never been a sparkling company. I got a lot of experience in industrial PR documentaries and I used whatever opportunity I had to turn them into pieces of impressionist art. They may not have always fulfilled their function, but they certainly were a good outlet for me.

My maternal grandfather made a great impression on me. He died when I was eight, but I can remember how we used to like going to his place because he made things. Towards the end, when he was not too well, his whole garden had run down. The lawns had become overgrown and all his hedges, which he liked to keep very trim and neat, had become rather dishevelled. So I went out and spent a whole day in his garden. I cut all the hedges, I cut a tree just outside the front door and I cut the huge pine hedge out the back. I was very pleased at the end of the day with what I'd done, and I thought I'd done it fairly well. Grandfather came out and all he said to me was: 'That's terrible!' And I just about burst into tears.

'What do you mean, it's terrible? I've done everything,' I said.

'You should have done that one tree only and done it perfectly, because you've done it all badly . . . You should have done just one tree and done it really well, and then I'd have been very pleased,' he said. That just hit me like a hammer. At the time I thought it was a terribly unjust thing to say. He should have just taken my childish enthusiasm and said thanks a lot. But I think that's had an incredible influence on me. I approach everything like that now. I would rather make just one film every four years and do it fantastically. If I am doing a commercial I can't just do it to throw it away; I have to put everything I've got into it.

Kerry Packer

Kerry Packer was born in Sydney on 17 December 1937, son of the late Sir Frank Packer, founder of the publishing and broadcasting empire, Consolidated Press. Kerry Packer is now the Chairman and Managing Director of the corporation his father created, and rules over a company that publishes magazines, including Women's Weekly, Cleo, TV Times, The Bulletin *and, most recently,* Australian Playboy.

Packer's company owns or has an interest in eight radio stations and five television stations throughout Australia, including Channels 9 in Sydney and Melbourne.

Kerry Packer shocked the cricketing world in 1977 when he contracted thirty-five of the world's top cricketers to play professional cricket for his World Series Cricket. At a stroke he acquired the Australian Test team for what became known as 'Packer's Circus'. With night matches, showmanship and clever 'C'mon, Aussie, C'mon' advertising, his company revolutionised the game, offending some traditionalists and delighting many who preferred the more flamboyant presentation of the contests. Frustrated in his attempts to secure the exclusive television rights to the traditional Tests and Sheffield Shield matches, Packer had retaliated by buying his own teams. After a disastrous attempt to play Test cricket without the players Packer had contracted for W.S.C. the Australian Cricket Board capitulated in 1979, giving the Packer organization exclusive television rights to Test cricket in return for the services of the cricketers who had joined World Series Cricket.

To tell about my childhood I must, right at the beginning, say something about my father. I believe that in every generation there are great and outstanding men, and that perhaps there were sixty or seventy or one hundred other men born in Australia about the same time as my father who were capable of creation. They're not always lovable or understood by the public, but for a man to be great he has to have a lot of compassion and understanding. He's usually busy, and that creates conflicts. But, nevertheless, my father was a great man. The best way I can describe such men is to say that there are any number of people who can go out and fly a jumbo jet, but there's a very elite group of people who can design it and make it work, and my father was a designer and a person who could make things work. If I've had any success it's because I was able to fly the plane he built, but I couldn't have built it.

My father built Consolidated Press from nothing. At about twenty-odd years of age, when he was a journalist, he got what he was going to get as an inheritance, which was, I think, about ten thousand quid and he came out and started Consolidated Press. He got lucky, and nothing works in life without luck. It's the ultimate thing and the greatest man in the world gets nowhere without it. He should have gone broke, but he had lucky breaks and things fell for him the right way.

So, what was my father? What were my feelings towards him? I was a bit scared of him. He was a strong man. He was a just man. I remember in my early life (he was a great believer in corporal punishment, as I am) he took me aside and said: 'Sometimes I have a bad day at the office and I'm angry. I'm going to come home, and if you believe that what you've done isn't worthy of the punishment that I decide you should have, you can have a stay of execution. All you've ever got to say is, "Look, I think you're in a bad mood and I'd like to discuss it with you tomorrow, and that'll stop it." ' He said that it may not alter the punishment—that he may decide on the next day that I was wrong and he was right—

but I had that option. And for a man who was supposed to be tough I don't ever remember one occasion on which I used the stay of execution. I got a lot of hidings, because that's the sort of person I was and the sort he was. I don't ever remember getting one I didn't deserve and there's a stack I didn't get that I should have got.

He wasn't a family man—he was a creator and he paid the penalty of all those who create. He devoted up to twenty hours a day to his business until he had built it. There are a lot of stories about him being a tough, hard man who wandered around the building turning lights off. And I'm sure you've heard the stories about how he used to personally sign the petty cash dockets. He did all those things for the reason that he never knew if he was going to have enough money at the end of the week to pay everyone. Those were habits which became ingrained in him for the best of reasons: he had to survive. They became something that was a bit funny when things weren't that tight, but he couldn't help it at that stage. I don't want you to think of him as a mean man; he wasn't. He was probably the most generous man that I've ever met, but he believed that you run a business as a business and you run it efficiently, and you run it tight and you run it hard. But in personal life he was the most generous man. If any of his friends had a problem or needed help he was always the first man there. Very quietly. I think he believed and I believe (I'm sure I got it from him) that if you were lucky enough to have a few bob then you should be as hard as is right within the organisation but if you're mean with it in your personal life then you're the lowest form of animal life. You divide yourself into a personal life and a corporate life, and in the personal life you've got friends. You can't get blood out of a stone—if a bloke hasn't got any money and doesn't shout that's because he can't afford to, not because he doesn't want to.

My father had a lot of influence on me in my early life. It would be pretty presumptuous to claim that I inherited any of his charac-teristics. I'm a great believer in the effects of environment. I was lucky enough to see my father running the business. I saw him run the telephone to the office every time I was home for twenty-three or four years. I saw his decision-making processes. When I came to work at eighteen I had already been exposed to the business for twelve years. That was what the house revolved around. Whatever concessions had to be made to be efficient within that business area I'd seen him make them. His attitude was that the job comes first and you've just got to get it done and it doesn't matter if it's three o'clock in the morning. I think it's a tremendous edge for anybody who starts off in life to see that sort of thing because it allows them to understand that you don't get there just by luck. You get there by being lucky but then accepting your luck and trying to make it work.

I went to boarding school in Sydney when I was about five for a short time and then when people thought the Japanese invasion was imminent I was sent to live with my mother's sister and two kids in Bowral and I went to school there. It was wartime, of course, and hard to get into a school, so I went to a girls' school with my aunty's daughters. I lived there for two years until one morning I got out of bed and just fell flat on my face. I had polio and rheu-matic fever and I was sent straight down to Sydney. They put me in hospital there for about nine months in an iron lung. I don't remember much about it except having lumbar punctures—that's the most vivid recollection. When I got over that and made a good recovery I was sent to Canberra, where the company had a place. The altitude was supposed to be the right thing for what I'd been through, so I was sent there with a nursing sister. I was lucky that my problem was diagnosed quickly and that I didn't try to strain myself, because I understand that's where the damage is done. But I couldn't walk and they thought I was trying to get out of school, because I loathed school.

146

I was academically stupid and my way of surviving through school was sport. I used to play everything. I was never a great natural talent, but I worked hard at all the sports that I played and I became reasonably competent at all of them. There's no point in being stupid about it—I've got a good ball sense, whether it be from playing polocross to tennis, cricket, to football, whatever it is. I lived my life for sport.

In Canberra, where I was looked after by the nursing sister, I went to a public school but I was obviously behind in my work. Then they got me into Canberra Grammar for a while and at the end of two years I came back to Sydney and that's really the first time that I remember living with my parents. For the four years since I had been sent to Bowral I had seen nothing of them, except for seeing my mother perhaps half a dozen times. It was the war and my father was working for the army and my mother worked hard in the Red Cross. It wasn't a matter of their not wanting to see me, it was a matter of getting on and doing things, which is something that I believe was right. I think they had to.

The most influential adult in the first few years of my life was my mother's sister, Mary Horden, who was a wonderful woman. After that there is a vacuum. The nurse, who was a nice woman, didn't really have a lot of influence. That was a fairly lonely, difficult period. Then when I went back to my first school, when I returned to Sydney, I was hopelessly behind everyone else and became a bit of a laughing stock because of it. My method of fighting against that was to devote myself to sport, where I had more ability than most.

Being an academic failure was very painful and this was a very tough period for a kid. It was probably the hardening of the shell, because kids are pretty unkind to kids. After a few years at Cranbrook, where I wasn't doing very well, I went to Geelong Grammar on the recommendation of the headmaster of Cranbrook. He said that we should try to get into Perry House because that was run by a man called Tunbridge who, I believe, is one of the giants of the education system. As fine a man as I've ever met, tough as billy goat's knees but dead straight. I've got great admiration for Tunbridge and he was obviously very influential in my life. I don't know that he'd be proud of my saying that, because I don't think the things I stand for are the things he stands for, but he became an influence.

I was twelve or thirteen when I went to Geelong and I used to see my parents only at the holidays.

My mother was one of four daughters in her family and a woman of beauty and intellect. She was devoted to her husband. He came first, as is right. I don't mean by that that she neglected us—she didn't. She believed that her function in life was to look after my father and I don't disagree with that. I think you do what you can for children, but you don't want to devote your life to them. When they grow up, as they must, and move away from you, as they should, an enormous vacuum appears. So I didn't really see much of my mother or father until I left school.

I had a disrupted childhood, which was nobody's fault. It wasn't a matter of neglect, it was a matter of circumstances. My father worked bloody hard to survive and I didn't see him because he paid a price for success. That price had to be paid in the Consolidated Press building in long hours. He had a morning paper, and that meant he used to go in there until eleven o'clock at night and of course he used to sleep in to nine o'clock in the morning, by which time I'd be at school. It wasn't that he didn't adore us, he did. Life's like a see-saw to me: if you get it *that* end, then you've got to pay for it *this* end, because one side goes up and one goes down. And he was a competitor; he couldn't help it. He had to get in there and fight.

How do I bring my own two children up? Well, funnily enough, I spend pretty long hours in the Consolidated Press building too. I want them to know only one thing, really—that I adore them. I'd do anything for them and they know that. They know they're loved. They're excited and happy to see me as I am to see them. That doesn't mean I don't put them over my knee—I do, but I hope fairly and never in anger. It's a belief that when you've done something wrong you've got to pay a price. Then we talk about it after it happens and say, 'It's paid now, but let's learn the lesson and not do it again.' My children have been lucky in life. I have a wife who has brought the children up and she's done a fine job. They really are great kids. I'm very proud of them and I'm proud of her, because she's the one who's done it. You're very lucky in life if you've got good kids and a good wife.

The quality or characteristic which I think I have learned from my father and other people who have influenced me, which I think is important, is loyalty. You have to give loyalty in order to receive it. I believe you offer loyalty to everyone, which is not as big a strain as it sounds, because very few people pick it up. It's a two-way street. It's looking after one's friends when it is inconvenient or difficult for you to do so. Anyone can look after someone if it's no problem, but it's real loyalty when you have to choose between something which you wanted or wanted to do, and their need. Then you have to choose to serve their need. I believe that's above everything else. You kid yourself if you think you can buy loyalty. You can't. You earn it through consideration and through being there when other people need you, regardless of what other commitments you have. I believe that you've got to be true to your beliefs, loyal to your friends and be a winner.

As I said before I know full well that I couldn't have done what my father did, build a great enterprise from nothing. I don't have those talents. I realised early that it takes a certain type of man to do what he did and I don't look at myself as a failure because I can't measure up to him. He was one of the exceptional people and I think you're damned lucky if you know one and you've seen how they operate. Just having known such men gives you a tremendous edge, which in itself should be enough without ever trying to aspire to be what they are, because you won't be. You'll fail, and that's the thing that cuts people around—the fact that they think they could have done what their father could have done, and not realising that it is a gift which is given to very few people. Don't feel ashamed if you're not given it.

My father was a gambler. Every man who ever created anything was a gambler. I am also, but there's a difference. What I risk on World Series Cricket is not going to put this company into jeopardy. It's not going to send it broke. I could close it down and the place would not even hiccup. What my father did was to take everything he had, all the prospects of everything he ever had and put it on one roll of the dice. And what happens with great men and creators is that they work so hard with so little. They're always undercapitalised at the beginning and they take the most outrageous risks. Against all the odds, and with luck, they survive. Then eventually they get to an age where they've built something and they sit back and say: 'I've done it!' And the next risk comes along that thirty years ago they would have pounced on, and they say, 'I don't want to put everything on another roll of the dice'; and they get conservative. Maybe they feel they're not young enough to do it again. They don't want to play the game any longer, but to sit down and consolidate. Then, in their offspring is the same type of conservatism. They too don't want to risk everything. Now I might risk more than the next guy, but I've never risked the lot. I've never risked anything that's going to put Consolidated Press at risk; might knock it around for a year or two, but we don't take the sort of risks where everything depends on it going right.

I believe I was a pretty lucky child. I was born with all the advantages—all the good things that could happen to me did happen. I had a bit of sickness, but how lucky I was to be able to get the right doctor. How lucky I was to be able to get into the right hospital. How lucky I was that I wasn't left with any scars. I can't tell you *the* happiest memory of my childhood, but I was lucky enough to have fantastic parents. Not in the run-of-the-mill interpretation of 'fantastic', but parents who, I think, had qualities which one was very lucky to see.

If I have one unhappy memory of childhood it was the loneliness. The opportunity to make friends wasn't there. I was continually moving, and even a couple of good friends I made at Geelong live now in Victoria, so I don't see them and we have obviously drifted apart. So I don't have friendships from school that go right back, because I was never there long enough, and that's a hard part of my recollections. Some of the holidays were lonely because of those sorts of things, but that is the luck of the draw. If I hadn't been sick and there hadn't been a war on it mightn't have worked out that way. But it did work that way and I don't feel lonely now. I've got a few mates who are very important to me, whose company I like, whose opinion I respect and whose friendship I value.

Then I suppose one could say that there's maybe one or two people out there who don't approve of me, but my early existence insulated me against those people pretty well. Maybe that was the way it was meant to be.

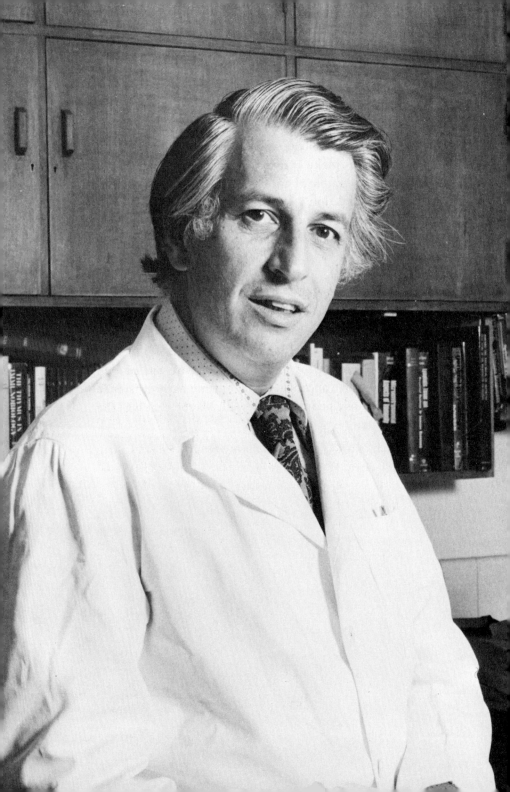

Gus Nossal

Professor Sir Gustav Nossal is one of Australia's most distinguished scientists. He is Professor of Medical Biology in the University of Melbourne and Director of The Walter and Eliza Hall Institute of Medical Research in Melbourne where the pioneering work was done in immunology which led to Sir MacFarlane Burnett's Nobel Prize. Sir Gustav was involved in that research. His honours and awards from Australian and foreign academic institutions include recognition from Germany, Israel, the U.S. and the U.K. He has held visiting professorships at universities in New York, Paris and Berkeley, California. He has lectured in Japan, Scandinavia and Belgium as well. He is recognised internationally as a leader in his chosen field of research in immunology which has been an essential factor in making organ transplants possible. His interests include broadcasting, music and education, and he is active in all these areas. From 1974 to 1977 he was a member of the international group of scientists known as 'The Club of Rome' which produced the controversial book, Limits to Growth. Sir Gustav has 236 scientific publications to his credit on immunology, cancer research and related topics. He has written three books, one of which has been translated into German, Italian, Russian and Japanese.

I was born in Austria in June 1931 and came to Australia in the early months of 1939, a migration forced on us by Hitler and his racist policies.

My parents were both Viennese. My mother came from a very old Catholic family that was very well established in Vienna and well known in government and diplomatic circles. My father was Jewish, but I have to qualify that direct statement. He was 'of Jewish extraction', as one would say today. His parents were a merchant banking family, and I think came to the realisation round about the turn of the century that to be Jewish in Middle Europe at that time was a social disadvantage. As far as I can tell they were not religious people and were never particularly interested in practising their faith, and they took a decision that many people of about that time took. My dad was born in 1893 and in about 1900 to 1905 they took the decision to have their children converted. There were two boys, my father and my Uncle Bob, and the decision was taken to have these two children baptised. Now, to give an indication of just how superficial this decision was in terms of any deep spiritual meaning attaching to the baptisms, they figured that the Catholic religion was fairly demanding—you had to go to Mass on Sundays and you couldn't eat meat on Fridays and so forth—so, in spite of the fact that 95 per cent of all Austrians are Catholic, they took the decision to have my father and his brother baptised into the Lutheran religion, which they believed to be less demanding. So my father was brought up as a Christian and educated in a snobbish, well-regarded Catholic school by Benedictine monks. When he grew up he didn't think of himself in any particular or deep sense as Jewish.

My father married twice, once during World War 1 as a young man to a Jewish girl. That marriage didn't work out and ended in divorce quite soon thereafter, and he married my mother when he was aged thirty. She, as I said, was Catholic. I believe that it would be fair to say that at the time this caused a certain amount of comment in what you might call snobbish Austrian circles, because my mother did come from a very 'good family', where it was not usual to marry someone of Jewish extraction. In fact she was a titled person, Baroness Loewenthal, but I must qualify that. In Austria, under the Hapsburg empire, there was a peculiar system under which all children of anyone titled carried the title. Now, there would have been a great-great-grandfather of mine, or perhaps an even more distant ancestor—who knows?—who was honoured for military service, then all the offspring, on both sides, male or female and whether married or not, carried on with the use of that title. So my mother would have been termed 'minor nobility', but she did come from a well-established family. Anyone who was anyone in Austria knew her father, because he was the so-called Kabinettdirektor, which, as closely as I can judge, was equivalent to Secretary to the Prime Minister's Department here. He was a highly regarded public servant. So that's why I say the marriage caused a little bit of a scandal.

My mother had in fact also had an unsuccessful marriage when she was very young. She married when she was sixteen and that marriage ended in divorce three or four years later. So both my parents were married for the second time, but fortunately their marriage proved to be a very stable one and they were together for thirty-eight years, I think it was, before my dad died. Mother is still alive.

This matter of being Jewish and not being Jewish meant that my father kept procrastinating on the whole question of what to do about Hitler's Germany. The *Anschluss* with Germany came in 1938 and Austria became a satellite of Germany and I think it was when that happened that my father saw the writing on the wall, although his employment opportunities and practical capacity to live his life had been deteriorating since about 1936. He left it very late, and my uncle didn't leave at all. He also was married to a Christian woman and he in fact survived the war without being deported to a concentration camp. But unfortunately we lost my grandmother at Theresienstadt, one of the Nazi concentration camps. My uncle was lucky to survive and probably only did so because he was married to a Christian woman. In the crazy logic of Hitler's Nazi Germany there was an order: they did fully Jewish people before they did half-Jewish people and so on.

I can remember a good deal about the Hitler period in Austria, particularly the excitement and euphoria and the adulation of Hitler. I think it is to the undying shame of the Austrian people that they so rapidly and assiduously embraced Hitler. I admit they didn't have much option. That puny country with its 6 million people was up against the mightiest fighting force that had ever been assembled in history, with the capacity to wage fantastic invasions. At the time of the *Anschluss* I remember extremely well the evening that Hitler addressed the Austrian populace from the balcony of the Hotel Imperiale. There was a huge crowd there and my two brothers and I moved heaven and earth to persuade our parents to allow us to at least go down there like all the other little kids and their parents to listen to the speech and to chant and sing. Of course my parents didn't accompany us. They didn't feel that that was at all fitting, but they unbent enough to allow me to go with the cook. So I saw Hitler and heard him make his speech and then the populace chanted '*Sieg Heil! Sieg Heil!*' We were sufficiently doubtful about the whole thing, the way that a six-year-old child would be, that we chanted out of time. Imagine, the populace is chanting '*Sieg Heil!*' and if in your mind you are chanting '*Heil Sieg*' it will add up to the same thing but you can kid yourself that you're not with the mob, and I can remember that very clearly.

The second thing that I remember about that time is that all of the other little boys in the class had a picture of Hitler sitting on their bedside table, perhaps like one might previously have had a picture of the Virgin Mary or St Joseph. These pictures were freely available and quite cheap, but I was not allowed to have one. Most of the kids in my class—I was in first grade—wore a swastika in their lapel and I wasn't allowed to do that, either. But I did put a swastika on the inverse side of my lapel, not showing, where I could sneak a little look at it.

There was euphoria about Nazism and adulation of Hitler in the air that all the other kids in the class felt as something positive and that I obviously wasn't allowed to express. At the time of this Hitler Jugend movement there was an attempt to get grips on the minds of the young people and there was a lot of publicity and emphasis given to youth. There were comic strips extolling the virtues of the Nazi state, together with children's stories, like Superman stories, but about the wonderful German youth who had spied out a nest of spies. He would be a twelve-year-old boy and the spies were all members of the 'International Jewish Conspiracy'. I remember reading these stories with fascination and identifying with the young heroes who were saving the State. I think this is an indication of what a tremendously powerful tool publicity and getting into the mind of the child can be. Despite the fact that my parents' very lives were threatened and that they must have endeavoured to imbue us with negative feelings about Nazism, nevertheless the six- or seven-year-old boy with all the forces of society around him could not help but be influenced in another direction and could not help but be torn. We were being brainwashed into being pro-Hitler, there's just no doubt about that.

We left Austria in the closing days of 1938 and I imagine that my mother would have told us that we would leave while Hitler was in charge in Germany and Austria, and that we would come back as soon as it was over. Once this rather ghastly thought that my father would have to leave his country and his friends and that my mother would have to leave her parents and that my father would have to leave his mother, had been dealt with then the one thought in my father's mind was to get us as far away as possible. I can remember my father telling us in later years that Australia was chosen because it was the furthest place he could think of. But I think there was another factor in it: my father was a bit anti-American. He didn't identify with what he saw as the materialism of America, the worship of material things and material progress. He was a little old-fashioned in that sense. England and France, which some people chose, he regarded as not safe and Latin America was too much of a black box. My mother had contacts with the Catholic church in Australia, particularly, through her family, with the Papal Nuncio, and I think that made a difference. That meant at least there would be someone that they could turn to in the new country.

They certainly intended to return to Austria. There was no thought in anyone's mind other than that this lunacy would pass very quickly and that they would return to normal family life as soon as that peculiar emergency was over. In the event, of course, that turned out to be an unrealistic hope. After the war Austria was divided into four zones, under joint American, French, Soviet and English domination until the creation of a new republic. So in fact one couldn't have thought of returning in 1945. 1948–1950 would have been nearer the mark, and of course by that time the family had had ten to twelve years in Australia and going back was no longer a realistic possibility.

My father was, in the best sense of the word, an intellectual. He was in many ways a frustrated intellectual. He was a deep-thinking man who thought far more about the nature of life, the reason that we're here on earth, the question of whether there is a life after death, the question of the best way to live your life, than he did about the ordinary concerns of most people, like how to make a lot of money. He was a reading man. I can never remember my father other than with a book in his hands when he was in the home. He made a habit of coming home from work reasonably early and he spent endless hours reading, frequently the old philosophers. Nietzsche, Kant and Schopenhauer were trotted out to us as the three great German philosophers. There were eastern philosophers like Lao-tzu and Confucius whom he told us about, as well as the great Hindu religions. He was always quoting from Rabindranath Tagore for example, and from the Koran. He was tremendously interested in comparative religion.

I called him a frustrated intellectual, because although he was a clever man, he was an unschooled man, or at least a self-schooled man. He left school at the conclusion of his high school years, about 1912. He then attempted to establish himself as a merchant banker. Then came the war, and he fought with the Austrian army and at the end of the war he used some money his father had left him to set himself up in a small bank. He burnt his fingers very badly. There were recurring and unbelievable currency crises in those days and to be a merchant banker was playing with fire. In 1923 there was a particularly bad currency shake-out and he had gambled against the wrong currency. His partner, in fact, committed suicide at the time. Although my father went right to the wall he managed somehow, goodness knows how, over the next few years to repay all the creditors. He did the right thing, but by the middle of the 1920s he was out of any money that his father had left him and he had to remake his life. I can often remember my father saying to me that he wished that his father had lived. His father had died when he was sixteen and so he felt the lack of parental guidance. He strongly urged us from the very beginning to seek tertiary education, because only if you have a profession, only if you can think your way through things, only if you're a schooled and tutored person will you make a success in life. In a funny sort of way, even though he'd made a fair bit of money in Australia, he didn't really consider himself a success. He would much sooner have been a doctor or a lawyer. So he was a frustrated intellectual.

When he came to Australia he first set up business manufacturing, of all things, washing-up soap. What we used to call 'soft soap'.

He did it with a partner with whom he had a bust up and he lost a bit of money out of that. He had only a small stake when he came to Australia, maybe £2,000 or £3,000 that he was able to get out of the old country, virtually smuggle out, I suppose, and on the basis of that he advertised in a newspaper: 'Have a small amount of capital. Would like partner in business venture.' A chap called Fred Clark replied to his advertisement. Clark was in a very small way in the sheet metal business, mainly making coal scuttles. Then the war came. That was really a big help to anyone who was in that style of manufacturing industry. And shortly after that they cottoned onto the virtues of stainless steel. They grew substantially during the war through important, and I think helpful to the country, contracts. When the war was over they moved into the large area of stainless steel sinks, and were probably the largest manufacturer of stainless steel sinks in Australia when dad died in 1962. The war gave dad a lift along, he capitalised on it, he worked hard, he got competent technical people around him and he built the business into one which, by the end of his life, employed about 500 people.

My father was also a rather stern man. He was a person who believed deeply in discipline. He believed in non-materialistic striving and he had a gruff exterior. He was a person without too many friends—an inner person. The dominant remembrance of my relationships with him are of a kind and good man, but a man who would not intuitively warm to one. I'm sure that he was intensely fond of his children, but he found it extremely difficult to show that. Certainly in the younger years he was the disciplinarian who ticked us off when we had to be ticked off. There is a small number of people in Australia who knew him well and loved him dearly and thought of him as someone very special. There are far more people, I think, that would have said there goes a cranky old guy, we won't have too much to do with him.

I'm not like my father in a lot of respects because I tend to be more of the extroverted, gregarious type. But I think I have certainly inherited from him a love of scholarship and the love of using one's mind. So, if there is an intellectual tradition in the family a good portion of it would come from him. The discipline of sitting down and learning something and reading a lot I have from him. But in terms of basic character traits I am not like him. For example, he was much more single-minded than I am. One of my besetting sins, which may or may not also be a virtue, is that I'm rather broadly based. I have a lot of interests. He wasn't like that but was much more inclined to single-mindedly pursue particular goals. If this year's project was to really get to the bottom of Meister Eckhart he would read his way right through every work that Meister Eckhart had ever written.

My mother is a very different type of person and I know that both she and my father believed that this attraction of opposites is the essential on which a good marriage depends. There have been many theories about that, but I think it really did work out in their case. My mother is a very warm and human person. I think she wouldn't mind my saying that in the normal sense of the word she's not an intellectual. She's a person who, when she was young, loved everything that was bright and gay. She loved parties and going to the opera. Today she can still sing you any song from any opera that was written in the nineteenth-century repertoire. She would spend two or three evenings a week at the Vienna Opera with her father in her young life. She is charming. She certainly would have been attractive when she was young. Now, when I say that she's not an intellectual I don't want to say that she's stupid by any means. She is a well-read person, but whereas my father was well-read in non-fiction she'd be well-read in fiction. She loves reading whatever might be the latest novel, and I don't think she'd mind my saying that they would tend to be light novels rather than heavy.

As I said she is a person of great charm and personal warmth. I can remember when I was a kid going into town from the suburb where we lived in Sydney, about 20 kilometres from the city. We were going in to town in the train and she would always start off a conversation with the person sitting next to her and I would be, as a little boy, embarrassed because of her thick, foreign accent and I would wonder why she was making this fuss, talking to this person in a foreign accent, when she had nothing to do with that person at all. That's the type of person she is. Very keen in friendship. Very attached to her boys. I think she made the three boys the centre point of her life after the migration—not to the exclusion of my father, but perhaps she placed the boys even a little ahead of my father in terms of her interests and where her energies were going.

I'm like my mother in two ways. Firstly, in wanting to be liked. I think that's been a big feature of a lot of the things I've done on the science-in-society interface. Most scientists are remote and inner people. I'm the sort of person that wants to be liked by a group; who may even go quite a long distance in order to be liked; maybe, in some ways, too soft a person for some angles of the leadership role into which life and history have placed me. Then, secondly, I am like her in the sense that she will embrace a very wide variety of interests. She'll be wondering about a particular friend one minute, then her mind will flit off quite quickly to some other entirely different concern. My mind tends to be a little bit like that, wandering from point to point and I've got to discipline myself to keep my mind on an even track, on the single-minded goal.

I also look more like my mother. I've inherited her rather buck teeth, which on my mother look very charming. The thick black hair I also got from her. She has some Yugoslav blood as well as Austrian and she's got a very thick mane of black hair, which even today, at seventy-seven, is still only flecked with grey.

On the relative importance of genetic inheritance and environment in shaping a person I would have to say that the innate abilities that we've got, the real genetic potential to excel, is inherited.

162

But I think that inherited seed of potential can be greatly moulded by environment and by experience and the atmosphere in which you grow up. Let me tell you how I see this has worked out in myself.

We have a situation in which two mature people—my dad aged forty-five and my mother aged thirty-eight, had to leave their own country and come to Australia where they literally knew no one. Previously they had been well-established and well-regarded. Now they were intensely lonely and one could not imagine a more difficult thing than these two mature people in middle life having to re-establish in what was a very alien environment. They felt most acutely their cultural isolation. They felt that this rather colonial set of Anglo-Saxon types was very different from anyone they knew and in some respects inferior. Austria has a deep culture and they had their roots in music and literature. I think they might initially have found Australians to be a little boorish. What effect did this have on us three boys? There was a tremendous urge, particularly coming from my father, that the boys should be special, that they should succeed and that they should be rewarded if they did succeed. You've got to prove that the Nossals can take it in this kind of an environment. You've got to succeed and through that success establish your worth, and perhaps vicariously, the worth of the family. Now, I have no doubt that that was a major, if not perhaps *the* major force in those early years of my life.

When we settled down here and found somewhere to live my parents sent me to St Aloysius' College, the Jesuit school in Sydney. This was in 1939, when it was normal, even in grade 3, for every subject to be examined and for you to be marked from one to one hundred. You would also get a ranking in the class and the last boy in our class of twenty-six would, of course, be twenty-sixth. I can remember as if it were yesterday the exams at the end of my first term there. It was in May. I had been put into the school in April. I didn't speak a word of English and it is not surprising that I came twenty-sixth in the class, and I can remember that figure still. I can see it in front of my eyes now, leaping out at me from the page, because in Austria I had never had anything but good reports. I said to myself, 'Well, this is not too good.' And by the end of the second term I was first in the class. Now, I suspect that a good part of that *sturm und drang*, or call it what you will, is related to this need to succeed in the alien environment.

Let's not beat about the bush—if I hadn't in some sort of way been 'clever' (I don't even know what that word means) I don't think I would have ended up first in the class. So I think that particular constellation of qualities that makes you a quick learner, able to comprehend things easily, put facts together in a certain way, to my way of thinking is indubitably genetic. I don't think we know precisely what genes control it, although it is certain that it is a large number of genes conspiring together. But I think that intelligence in many kids will remain dormant or latent or not harnessed to some defined goal, while in other kids, shaped by parental and school influences, that potential will be realised into some kind of a success. My elder brother was also the sort of always-be-first-in-his-class type of kid and went on to university and became a biochemist. He died at thirty-three, but by that time he was a Reader at Adelaide University. My middle brother was also very successful, but he was not as study-oriented and he left school very young and became a journalist. He had no tertiary education, a lack which he still feels and blames my father for not having worked harder to make him go to university. But he is now a very successful journalist, working now with the World Bank in the information section. It must have been quite difficult for him, squeezed in as the middle brother of three, where the elder and younger did exceptionally well in his father's eyes. He was the more artistic type, always doing well in the school plays and operas and coming fifth or sixth in class rather than first or second.

My dad believed in rewarding the reports that one got with small amounts of pocket money. I think this was very bad psychology. If you got a very good report with first in every subject you would get 6 shillings, but if you got only a moderate report you would get 3 shillings, and this equation of reward with the particular achievement must have been quite difficult for my middle brother. There would be no way in the world that any kid of mine would ever be rewarded by money for having done well in an exam. One acts on the presumption that the kid goes in there to do his best. He is encouraged at all times to put good effort into the set duties and the reward is the smile on his father's face.

I was completely hopeless at all sport except ping-pong, unbelievably enough. I worked very hard at table tennis and got into the semi-finals of the junior championships in Sydney. But I was completely hopeless at all other sports—cricket, football, athletics— and that was quite a pain to me in childhood. I was also hopeless at music, unbelievably bad! I learnt the piano year after year without making any progress, much to my dear mother's distress, and finally was allowed to give it up. And I was equally hopeless, pathologically so, at anything to do with drawing. All the teachers, from every report that I can remember, commented on the abysmal lack of neatness in my work. I think that is genetic, too.

It sounds a funny thing to say of a divorced woman, but my mother was a good Catholic. She had this compromise that she had made in her life, but she was religious in the conventional sense and was a very devout woman, although because of the exigency of her marriage she couldn't practise her religion to the full extent. She couldn't go to Communion for example. In a funny sort of way my father was religious, too. He would think a lot about God and talk to us a lot about religious questions. But because he was not a devout Lutheran and my mother was a good Catholic and we were at a Catholic school we were brought up as Catholics in the fullest sense of that word. I remember being very positive about the Jesuits. Very devout. I was a pious little boy,

always going down on my knees saying prayers. I was very enthu-
siastic about all of the religious things like visiting the little grotto
where Our Lady's statue was exhibited. Things like Lourdes and
Fatima really turned me on. I have no hesitation in saying that
religion was a very important force in my life during all of those
school years. The Jesuits were excellent to us and I believe that I
owe them a tremendous debt. They took the children without
charge at the beginning, then, when my father was able to pay a
bit, they first levied for the three boys the equivalent of one normal school fee. Apart from anything else they provided a surround-
ing of stability and support when we most needed it and I can
genuinely say that my school years were undilutedly happy, being
shaded only by my abject hopelessness at all sport, which of course
made me a figure of some derision amongst the other boys, who
also didn't like someone who was a bit of a bookworm. But with
that small proviso I was extremely happy at school.

I must say that I have painful childhood memories that relate to
sex. You can imagine that with a strict Catholic upbringing there
was a particular association of anything sexual, outside marriage,
with guilt. As I was a very pious boy at the age of fourteen to sixteen this caused in me far more anxiety than it might have done in
many kids who were less pious. That's a common story, but I do
believe that that's changed, and changed for the better, in recent
times. I can divide up my childhood into three periods. The first is
the period in Austria of which the dominant recollections are of
odd little happenings and then the trauma and thrill of the Hitler
period and emigration. Then there's the period between arrival in
Australia and puberty, which with a couple of little ups and downs
was really happy. Then the period between puberty and young
adulthood, where this problem of guilt associated with sex I
remember as fairly dominant. That's something that I hope is not
quite as difficult for my kids as it was for the kids then.

I was often bored as a child. There would be times in class where a set of maths problems had to be coped with and I was lucky enough to be able to solve whatever it was in ten minutes, but the class took thirty-five minutes. There was just nothing to be done for the remaining twenty-five minutes. That was a fairly frequent experience for me and it has made me wonder about the whole question of streaming. Is it right that all kids should be together in a class, no matter what their IQ? Furthermore, is it right that the pace is the pace of the slowest, because there is no question that in those days that is how it was. I think that this is a very important and deep question, because in a strange way it carried over into aspects of home life. I didn't seem to have the gumption or drive to sort out for myself a rich intellectual life. There were other kids who learned how to use libraries very cleverly and perceptively. In my reading as a small boy I never got beyond the regular school stories and it wasn't until much later in life that I started to read serious things. So I can remember long periods of being bored, not unhappily bored, but nevertheless bored. I'd ask my mother, 'What'll I do now?' My kids aren't like that. As a matter of fact I'm surprised if they ask me anything!

I've got four children of my own, ranging in age from twenty-one to thirteen. I could see what a tremendous importance a stable family life and caring parents had on my own formation and so, very consciously but not with a great deal of effort, because it came naturally, I set out to create that kind of caring environment for my own children. I believe I'm terribly lucky, because at a time when other parents worry about drop-outs and drugs and the generation gap and so forth I've got four kids who are fine, stable normal sorts of individuals, who are all very different from each other and from my wife and myself. They care for each other and for their parents, and that I think in a way I owe to my own parents.

I can remember very clearly a little *bon mot* of my father, who was full of little wisdoms, like Confucius. He used to say: 'The man is the head of the family; the wife is the heart of the family.' I think he genuinely believed that and he was not alone in his generation. He believed that the chief decisions were made by the man using his intellect, and that the woman used her spirit, her soul, her goodness, the God-given qualities of succouring that is associated with femininity, to provide a heart and a hearth. I'm pretty sure that I took that kind of a concept into my marriage, which of course completely begs the question of the woman's intellectual development through marriage. I'm really talking about male chauvinist piggery versus equality in marriage. There's no way in the world that my father would have participated in or adhered to the Women's Lib movement. He had his own set and very traditional ideas about the role of women, and although I don't believe I ever articulated this, nor was it an issue that was much talked about in our day, I suppose subconsciously I carried those attitudes with me. Now it is really only through the act of being married and seeing how important it is that women should be allowed to pursue their own interests and goals and develop their minds and have all of the sorts of outlets that men do, that I have progressively changed my attitude. I think marriage is a straight 50-50 situation and should be a true partnership. It's hard for me to judge this, but I think in our marriage it is. I genuinely believe that I am no longer a male chauvinist pig, but that took quite some time!

I have attempted to explain to my children the association between effort and achievement—that if you really want something badly, you can have it, but you've got to work for it. The thing that I am not as sure about as my father was is putting so much emphasis on the purely intellectual side of that. I think this is a discipline of a general sort; if you want to be a good musician, if you want to be a good painter, if you want to be good at sport, you've got to work at it. I believe in that rather old-fashioned view and I've attempted to define it to the children. They say to me,

'But Dad, life's not just about work and achievement.' They've been very influenced by the trends of their times, the experiential bit. They're much less success-oriented than I am. They've got a very full and broad approach to life.

Clifton Pugh

Clifton Ernest Pugh was born on 17 December 1924. He is one of Australia's foremost artists, represented in all major Australian galleries and in the Royal Collection in Britain. He has won the Archibald Prize three times. One of his best known portraits is of former Prime Minister, Gough Whitlam, now hanging in Parliament House, Canberra.

Pugh has a deep affection for Australia's animals and at his home near Eltham in Victoria he has a very friendly but destructive wombat. His love of animals is evident in his illustrations for the books Death of a Wombat and Dingo King. Some years ago Pugh collaborated with photographer Mark Strizic to produce a book of portraits of famous Australians, with photograph and painted portrait of the same person on facing pages. The book was called Involvements.

Clifton Pugh is chairman of the Arts Policy Committee of the Victorian branch of the ALP. His most recent venture into popular art is the project that he conceived to commission artists to decorate Melbourne's elderly green trams. His own contribution to the project was so highly regarded that before the tram had even left the depot where it was being prepared one of the windows on which he had painted had been stolen.

Pugh lives with his wife Judith in a wonderful, rambling mud-brick house which he has built himself, beginning when he was discharged from the army in the late 1940s.

I was born in Richmond, Victoria in December 1924 and my earliest memories are of living in a big, two-storey house, virtually on the beach at Frankston. I was the youngest of three children, with my elder brother being about eleven years older than me and the middle brother being about five years older. This spacing of the children was partly caused by World War 1. My elder brother was born before the war, then the next was born when my father came back from the war and I think I was an accidental child; born, I think, on mum's 'change of life'.

When I was about four my father told me the old story about catching birds by putting salt on their tails. I was always wandering about the bush on my own, so I got a bag of salt from the housekeeper and out I went to try to catch some birds by putting salt on their tails. Very quickly I woke up to the fact that you had to catch the bird first. I remember I was so indignant at that. I lost all faith in my father, that he'd try to fool me like that. And I was indignant with myself that I didn't see through it in the first place. That annoyed me even at the age of four. I can still remember the resentment. I never forgave my father for that.

Because of the differences in ages with my brothers I was, in a sense, an only child. I was always on my own and always walking in the bush. Wherever we've lived, except for a short period in Kew, I have lived near the bush. We moved from Frankston to Kew and then to Greensborough where my father had a model farm. I've always been alone and I've always wanted to be alone, which I think affects all my relationships now, because I never really give over to someone else. That's why I've had so many wives, I think.

I've had three official wives and we're all still mates. That's another thing, I don't like losing people, so I sort of hold them all about. I've learned now the only way you hold people is by being nice to them!

My father was a disciplinarian. I remember once I'd broken a window while playing football, and I think my father must have come home in a bad mood. He wasn't usually a basher, but I remember this time he hoed into me and I shot under the bed. He kept belting me under the bed and mum came in and dragged him off.

My father had come to Australia from Wales just before the First World War, to bring the first motorised fire engine to Western Australia. As he'd been working on its design he was given the trip— bringing it out for the Western Australian Government, I suppose. He came out to demonstrate how it worked, and then stayed and married my mum. Later they came to Victoria where he was head draughtsman with the Victorian Railways.

When we shifted to Greensborough father had a 'model' farm. It was a hobby for him, not an early experiment in self-sufficiency. The orchard would have been an acre (0.4 ha) in size with two of every sort of fruit tree you could grow in the area. He had two cows, a couple of horses and chooks. He was always inventing things, and he developed the very first egg-washing machine that was ever invented. I've got a copy of it at home now. He invented a new concept for a sun dial and an *almost* perpetual motion machine!

Life on the farm was pretty hard in a way, because I used to have to get up at six in the morning in the middle of winter when I was about seven, eight or nine and cut all the green stuff for the chooks and milk the cow before I could go to school. Then I'd have to go and catch the ruddy horse and saddle it up and ride to school. This all took so much time that I remember my father bought me a secondhand bike, which was the thrill of my life at the time.

Before I had the bike I remember that I used to get threepence a week pocket money for doing the work and I used to ride the horse down to Greensborough, which was just a tiny little country town then, and buy a copy of *Champion* and an iceblock, and that took up the threepence. Then trying to get up on this huge horse, which was generally bareback, with an iceblock in one hand and *Champion* under my arm was a hell of a job. I had to back it up to a step or something so that I could get on without dropping the iceblock.

My father died when I was ten and I had no reaction to it at the time. I was never really close to him. He'd been up in Queensland for two years before his death designing a diesel rail motor. We remained on the farm until mother sold it a few months before dad died so that we could go to Queensland to live. We'd only been there a few months when he died and then we came straight back to Victoria. Mother tried to buy back the place in Greensborough and couldn't, so then we moved to Camberwell.

Up to this time we had been financially secure, then suddenly we had nothing. He must have poured all his money into the farm, but it was never a paying proposition. He was far too noble for this world and had signed away all his pension rights, and, even though he was gassed quite badly in the war, he signed away all his rights. He was fighting for 'God, King and Country', doing his duty. And as he was well off on a good salary right through the Depression he didn't think he should take money from the State for what he thought was his duty. Silly Welsh bugger! So he left mum with virtually no money at all, because she'd sold the farm cheaply, gone up to Brisbane and bought an expensive house, sold it again, I should think at a loss, and come back to Melbourne.

At first she sent me to Ivanhoe Grammar and she slowly had to sell items of furniture in the house to pay for my schooling. One of the things I remember very much was our big player piano. It must have been a wrench for her to sell that because she used to love playing it. She used to organise the school choir when we were at Greensborough and she used to have the kids from the school in on Sunday afternoons. She played the piano and they sang. I wasn't musical, so I wasn't involved in it, but I used to like listening to it. I remember I used to come home from school and mum would often be out, and I'd play the piano and sing like blazes. When it was sold it would have been a blow for her and it was also a very big blow for me. It was a very disruptive stage in the home with things being sold off.

Finally it came to an end and she couldn't keep me at school anymore. I left at thirteen. I loved school . . . I loved history, mathematics . . . I just loved going to school. But we were utterly, fearfully broke and I had to go out to work.

My mother, who is still alive and somewhere about ninety, came from Western Australia where her father was the government astronomer. Just before the First World War she did the 'Grand Tour' of Europe, with a little watercolour sketch pad. In fact both my mother and father used to paint in their spare time. Mum came from a very genteel family, but I remember her as being pretty tough. She was pretty hard . . . just, but hard. I don't remember any great cuddles or hugs. I don't think she was that sort of demonstrative person.

I remember when we had moved from Frankston to Kew and I could no longer go wandering into the bush or along the beach, where I used to spend all day on my own. Being conditioned to wandering off on my own I took to following the rubbish man for some reason, perhaps because he had a cart with horses. I used to ride with him all over the suburbs and my mother would have to find me. To stop my wandering she used to stake me out in the back yard. When she went out she'd tie me with a harness to a peg in the middle of the lawn, like a dog on a chain. I have great resentment about that because I was restricted and I hate being restricted.

I don't think we were a warm family. As I said, I don't remember any cuddles and hugs from my mum, but then I don't have any bad memories of her. Actually I seem to have quite a lot of respect for her and I like her. You see I'm not using the word 'love', and I certainly wouldn't for my father. I remember him only as a stern disciplinarian whom I didn't see much. Because of this family background I've tended to want to live my own life and make myself entirely self-sufficient. When I think back I led a very isolated life. I never really made close friends, preferring to be off wandering on my own. Later, when I was about sixteen, my mother shifted to Adelaide and I went to live there for a while and during my holidays I'd hire a horse, take my paints and go off and camp in the Adelaide Hills. With a horse, a tent and a groundsheet I'd wander about the country painting. Then later still, when I was in the army in New Guinea I used to piss off on my own. I always chose to be forward scout. I discovered all sorts of things the army was thankful for. I used to take a hell of a lot of risks out there on my own, wandering about behind Japanese lines. I was only happy when I was on my own, not because I was brave, it was because I couldn't stand walking behind anyone. It is honestly as simple as that. I just had to be in front.

All my happiest childhood memories are of wandering alone in the bush. I was very sad when we sold the Greensborough farm to go to Queensland. I didn't want to leave because there were a hundred acres (40 ha) of bush opposite us where I used to walk and study the birds and the orchids and the grasses. I knew every orchid and every bird in that patch of bush. It was there that I developed my affection for native plants and animals that now feature in my paintings.

I've wanted to draw all my life. At school I was always drawing, but of course art wasn't a subject on the curriculum in those days. In fact I didn't have any formal art instruction until I came back from the army when I was about twenty-one. But I was always drawing, as a child, and entering competitions like those run by the Young Herald League, I think it was called, and I had certificates all over the place. Then, when my father died, all his paints were left and that's when I actually started painting. My mother, as a sort of little family joke, used to tell fortunes with cards and by reading hands. I always remember that in telling the fortune from the cards you had to make a wish before they were cut. Consistently, even as a young kid, I remember I always had two wishes, to be prime minister or a painter. Over the years I've dropped the prime minister and settled for the painter.

When I left school at thirteen it was still the Depression but I got a job as an office boy in a paper called the *Radio Times*. It was a radical left-wing paper, which caused my mother a lot of concern. I used to do drawings and kids' competitions for the paper, I remember. In fact I've still got them. One of my jobs was to take material down to the Censor's Office and I was once set-up, not deliberately, but I was sent down with some material while other copy that they wanted to print but wouldn't have passed the censor, they kept back. It was political and I was the patsy. The police raided the *Radio Times* and we were all held, locked in the office, for the whole weekend while they questioned us. My mother read the writing on the wall and got me out, and not long after the paper closed. She used her husband's past contacts and got me a job in the draughting office of the aircraft factory at Fisherman's Bend, which was awful. I hated it. Even though I was supposed to be in the draughting office I was actually in the factory and I couldn't stand the noise. Not long after I went to Adelaide.

In Adelaide I went to the very first exhibition of contemporary Australian art and I was so excited. I can still remember the absolute excitement of seeing those paintings. There were Arthur Boyd's and Percival's and early Tucker's and early Nolan's. I came raving home to my mother. Then she went in to see it and was horrified and immediately bought me a book of Raeburn portraits, which is the height of conservatism, and that was something that also made me realise that while I suppose I was close to my mother there was something that made a rift there. I thought, 'You just don't understand!' Obviously she had a very directing influence on my life, but trying to push me always in a different direction. She always aided me in painting, never the slightest hindrance to that, but she tried to direct it in a particular channel which she approved of.

I now have two children of my own, two sons, one twenty-six and the other about twenty-four. It's a bit late, but I'd love to have a family over again now, because I've learned so much. I'm trying now to break down that self-sufficiency that prevented me getting really close to people, because I think I've missed out on something worth a lot. I think now I'd be a very good, warm, affectionate father. Maybe because I'm more secure, I don't know. I was so busy when I started painting, and it seemed there was no way that I was going to make a living from it, but I determined never to work more than two days a week for wages and the rest of the time I'd paint. The two children were with my second wife, and I don't think I was much good as a father because I was much more concerned with my painting. I always used to say to Marlene —poor lady—that there are three important things in my life: the most important is my art; then there's you; and then there's the kids. I used to lay it down the line to her. I wouldn't say that now. It happens to still be true, there's no way I wouldn't paint, but I used to actually lay it down the line to her. So the kids came even after Marlene—I couldn't have been that good! Yet they seemed to be very affectionate and warm towards me, so obviously I wasn't that bad, either, but I don't think I was a great warm, cuddly, nice father. I'd take them to the football, on principle, a couple of times, but I wasn't interested. I'd rather be home painting.

Now that I'm older and perhaps I've matured I think I'd be a better father. I'm usually a late goer at these things, particularly in emotional and social matters—I was a very late developer. Always. But I have no regrets.

George Dreyfus

George Dreyfus is one of Australia's best known and most prolific composers. His theme music for the ABC television series Rush earned him instant fame, considerable income from its 100,000 record sales and a Television Society Penguin in 1975.

From 1953 to 1964 Dreyfus was bassoonist with the Melbourne Symphony Orchestra. Since then he has established his reputation as a composer of symphonies, chamber works, television music, film themes and operas. The World Record Club has released a record of his music for Break of Day, Rush, Marion, Power Without Glory, A Steam Train Passes and other film and television music. His Symphony No. 1 and his Sextet For Didjeridu and Wind Instruments have also been recorded. He works very hard at being interesting, as he himself claims, and is a tireless and charming self-promoter. On his own record label, Three Feet (a literal translation of his name) he has released a recording of his one man show, George Dreyfus Live. And to children he is probably best known for his music Sebastian The Fox, written for Tim Burstall's television series of that name.

George Dreyfus has studied bassoon at the Vienna Academy of Music and has won a UNESCO scholarship, a Creative Arts Fellowship of the Australian National University and the Prix de Rome, German Academy in Rome. He was commissioned to write music for the Australian contribution to Expo '70 in Osaka.

His latest venture in film music is for the 1979 production of Dimboola, for which he has written an amusing score for brass band.

181

I was born on 22 July 1928 in Wuppertal, which is in the Rhine-land, roughly 45 kilometres from Cologne. It's an industrial town in the Ruhr where my father was a scrap-metal merchant with a prosperous business with a number of employes.

Being Jewish my father was forced to sell his business and we went to live in Berlin from 1936 to 1939. One reason why we moved was because we couldn't get permission to go to the state school in Wuppertal and the nearest Jewish school was in Cologne, which was too far to travel in the train every day. Anyway, after the business had been sold there was no reason to stay in Wupper-tal and my father thought it would be safer in a bigger city. Ulti-mately, once war was declared, it was all the same. But in 1936, when there was sporadic anti-semitism—riots, burnings, daubing of shops—one thought it was safer in the big cities, so we moved to Berlin. We lived in the Toorak of Berlin, Dahlem. My father had money (I would say that he sold the firm twice, once for the official money and then for the unofficial money). We had a cook and a children's maid, but after the Nuremberg laws said that women working in Jewish homes had to be above a certain age to avoid adulteration of the race, and that Jewish homes were only to have one servant per household, the children's maid disappeared and there was only the cook. The cooks were always quite old and forever changing because of the pressures not to work in Jewish homes. But still there would always be this other presence in the house.

Very rarely did we have meals as one family. Children ate first, you see. Then when my father came home to sleep we had to keep the whole house very quiet. These things, which sound abnormal now, were completely normal then.

I remember very little of my earlier life in Wuppertal. I can recall tobogganing in the steep side streets and being annoyed that they'd spread salt on the streets so that the cars could drive but we couldn't do our tobogganing. I can always in my mind's eye remember seeing the first aeroplane. I was in kindergarten and everybody was pointing up at the plane flying over. But apart from that my memories of Wuppertal are nil. Later I remember crying in the opera and having to be taken outside because I was frightened of the witch in Hansel and Gretel. And I couldn't be taken to the movies, ever, because they frightened me terribly and I always had to be taken outside. I don't want to talk about it—but I was not very bright.

We left Germany just before the war, my brother and I on 10 June 1939 and my parents on 1 August. War was declared on 1 September.

My father held out as long as he could, thinking himself to be utterly assimilated, being proud of his Germanness. He was a very Germanised, very cultured man. An excellent pianist. Before television and radio lay music-making was very strong in central Europe and my father was particularly good in Lieder companies. He was a very musical man, but as he had wealth it was not done to be a professional musician.

Before the war the Nazis' aim was to get as many Jews as possible to leave the country, leaving behind their assets. The programme of extermination came later. So, why did some leave when they had the chance and others didn't? We don't really know. I've since heard a story about my mother's father going around after the war started banging his his hip pocket and saying: 'I have my money—they won't touch me.' Little did they know! He died in the Theresienstadt 'model ghetto'. My father's mother, who was still living in Wuppertal, received her notice to pack her bags and she took poison and was found dead next day. My mother's mother got her orders to present herself to the police in Wiesbaden and she apparently died in the police station there.

It was a characteristic of cultured German families to have evenings of chamber music. House music, it is called. It's the equivalent of standing around the piano here singing 'Roll out the Barrel . . . '

but in Germany it wouldn't be associated with grog and a good night out, but it would be about Schumann and Beethoven Trios and Schubert Lieder. We children were allowed to come in, sit down, not say a word and listen. It was all part of our education, very strongly emphasised in the German way of life. I liked music, but I wasn't very good at it. I learnt the piano but I gave it up because I couldn't get the left hand and the right hand to play together!

I didn't have a brilliant relationship with my father. He was really quite strict, but pointlessly strict. There was perpetual confrontation without any reason except that that was the German tradition. My wife Kay and I were living at the German Academy in Rome for three months recently and it's still the same. Children are brought up differently. It has affected the way I dealt with my own children, who left the house with my first wife when they were six, and with whom I've got a fabulous relationship now. I didn't do much bringing up at all, except when my wife was ill with asthma, and then I tended to be a bit too strict. I didn't know any other way of being brought up, but it's not my way of thinking today. The German situation was very heavy with a tradition that children must be seen and not heard.

My mother over-compensated with love. She was utterly devoted to her two children and I think she was probably very soft with us to compensate for my father's stricter disciplinarianism which caused nervous tension in the home. She is a nice, charming person, and I understand, very beautiful when she was young. She came from a wealthy family and was an only daughter. She did have a sister, but she died very young. She has adjusted well to the trauma of coming to Australia. The change wasn't easy for her: from a life of luxury in a big house with servants to life here where she was the servant. She got off the plane here and had to start work cleaning houses and flats and working in fruit shops.

As a child I was aware of anti-semitism, but I was introverted, not an outgoing person at all, and my reaction was that it's not touching me, which would be quite normal I would say. But I do remember, as I said before, that we couldn't get permission to go to school in Wuppertal. Then, when we moved into our posh house in Dahlem, I remember there was a shop down the street which had a sign 'Jews Not Welcome'. There was a little inner torment. And we had to carry indentification papers, which Germans always do, even to this day. We had to go to the local police station to have the word 'Israel' put in our identification papers, because the law said that all German-Jews had to have another name—something like Rebecca or Rachel for women or Abraham or Israel, for men. I'd been in school two or three years and I still couldn't write my name. I spelt Dreyfus with an 'i' instead of a 'y' and my father was furious. So I was not so much upset with getting a new name as with getting *ohrfeige,* which means a slap on the ear. It's very characteristically German. We also got *ohrfeige* at school, which I remember in Berlin.

We were not observant Jews at all, until the last year in Berlin when my father would light the candles some Friday nights. But these were just little turns of insecurity. He was a Zionist, but he didn't want to go to Palestine because living conditions there weren't that brilliant in 1939. He had been to Palestine in 1935 for the Maccabiah Games as a soccer umpire. And while we were living in Dahlem he worked in the Palestine Office set up to assist Jews who wanted to go to Palestine, leaving their assets behind, of course.

In Berlin I went to a Zionist school called the Herzl School, after the founder of Zionism. It's gone now—burnt down. We learnt a bit of Hebrew there, but apart from that it was a normal school. I was never any good at school. There was nothing I could do, arithmetic or anything. I went there until, bit by bit, things were getting worse, and the school was closed down. In the masterly German bureaucratic way the gradual process of the destruction of the Jews ground on. The Herzl school was closed and we had to go to the Grunwald school, perhaps the last remaining school with Jewish connections which in fact was non-political and non-sectarian. I had to take an oral entrance test, for which I was put in a classroom on my own, except for the examiners, and they pulled down a hunting scene and I had to talk about it. I can remember just as I was leaving I put my head back in the door and said, 'By the way, for your information I'm going to Australia next week.' I think that this realisation that I was leaving Germany was all a bit of a relief, because I was no good at anything because of the very traumatic times we were living through and were aware of but couldn't identify as the cause of my problems.

Originally my father had tried to save as much of the property as possible, but after a while some people's attitudes changed and they said, 'Hang the property. I'll save myself.' My father arranged for my brother and me to come to Australia on a children's transport. I think he bribed someone to get us on it—or at least he paid a huge sum of money to the Jewish organisation in Berlin in order to get us on to this transport which was essentially for children of underprivileged Jewish people who had no hope of getting out themselves. It was very difficult to get into Australia. It was during the Depression and my parents actually had to prove that they had a large sum of money, perhaps £1,000 in a bank in Sydney or Melbourne, before they got their visas. They were able to do this through friends who were already established here. Anyway, my brother and I got the train in Berlin in June 1939 to Bremen to catch the boat to Australia. A couple of days before we left my parents had also got their permits to leave, so, unlike most of the other twenty-odd children on the boat, we expected to see our mother and father again. I celebrated my eleventh birthday on the boat.

We chose to come to Australia because of the goodwill which came from the Jewish community in Melbourne. I don't know too much about this, but it seems the Jewish Welfare Agency in Mel-

186

bourne arranged for Jews to come here, through the many agencies that were in existence in Germany from the Nazi days onwards to try to save the Jews. When we arrived here we were met, not only by representatives of Jewish Welfare but also by two friends of my mother who came into the cabin and said, in German, 'How are you Georgie?' Very reassuring! Then we were taken to the Jewish Children's Home in Balwyn, where we stayed until our parents arrived and had found themselves a flat, which was in the early part of 1940.

Because they had money which they couldn't bring with them, my parents spent it on an airline ticket to Australia. Firstly they flew around Europe saying goodbye to friends and then got on a boat in Trieste, sailing to Palestine. From there they flew by KLM, taking a fortnight, I think, to Sydney and from Sydney to Melbourne by train. I remember meeting them at the station.

The day after my brother and I arrived, not speaking any English, we were put straight into school. There were no migrant services then, but it didn't take us long to learn the language because we weren't in the family environment, where German would still have been spoken, but in the children's home where we had to speak English. So we learnt very quickly. But in any case I did better in school here than I had in Germany. Perhaps the standard wasn't as high, but I think it was the release of tensions, you know. I think the tension in Germany must have affected me and made me introverted, which I can only say is a normal reaction, to be self-protective like a plant. Introversion would have been the easy way out of a tense situation. Anyway, I was a slow learner. But after coming to Australia I changed. I could do maths in my sleep. I surprised everybody. I became just the opposite of what I had been in Germany—very extroverted, very noisy, actually. I really underwent a complete change of character at the age of eleven.

I went to Melbourne High School, where I was always in anything. There were a number of gifted musicians there and we used to play chamber music. I was conductor of the House choir. I was always playing music, very badly, and arranging things. I was just busy. Bit by bit the music got a stronger hold and there was an ongoing battle beween my father and mother. I could have left school after doing Merit, but my mother had some feeling for soul over money and she didn't want me to go into my father's carpet-cleaning business. Although they had no money for piano lessons, and as I said before, they did no good, she worked extra at cleaning or nursing or in the greengrocer's shop so I could have my lessons. She had faith in my being cultured—not a musician—just *cultured* When I got to Melbourne High School I joined the orchestra as a clarinet player. It was my big thing. I bought my own clarinet and I was always playing in amateur orchestras somewhere. Then there were too many clarinet players around so I got a bassoon and then there were more avenues for playing. Both my mother and father encouraged that—they were very pleased.

They arrived in Australia simply pleased to be alive, even though they were exchanging wealth and luxury for initial poverty. They were just pleased to be alive, that was the overpowering feeling. My father went into the army in the Labour Corps, working on the railway at Albury and Tocumwal where the rail gauge breaks and trains from Melbourne and Adelaide had to be unloaded and reloaded onto the Sydney trains. They slept on the football ground at Tocumwal. They had uniforms, but no weapons, of course. My father was invalided out after a time and drove a delivery van for an engineering firm that made aeroplane parts. Then he bought himself a partnership in a carpet-cleaning firm with another Jewish man. We lived in a two-room flat, just bedroom and livingroom-kitchen in St Kilda. My father became exhausted and he was always depressed, unlike in Germany where he was always a fabulous fellow I am told by his old friends. He died in 1951.

My mother had attended synagogue a few times in Berlin, and when we arrived in Australia it started to play quite a big part in our lives. The synagogue became my communal life, actually. I sang in the choir; I was getting ready for my Bar Mitzvah, so it was a very, very important part of my life. At least it was until I started playing in the amateur orchestra that played on Saturday mornings. I remember the time I went to the rehearsal of the junior symphony orchestra on the Day of Atonement. We were living around the corner from the synagogue and I was slinking down the road wondering where to hide my clarinet case.

Now I like to think that my talent is really having something that's of interest to other people. I enjoy performing but I'm not really a Barry Humphries or a Norman Gunston. But I think people want to see composers a bit more now. Being an extrovert helps, as it helped me when I got thrown out of the Melbourne Symphony Orchestra which was a sudden release. I could do anything I liked, because I could only fail myself. I couldn't lose my income because I didn't have any.

I treasure a letter I have from an advertising agency who approached me about doing television commercials for carpets. They wanted to do ads with a personality and an orchestra, so I went to see them and played them some tapes of themes I had written and they sent me a letter saying I had too much personality! 'Dear Mr Dreyfus, You have too much personality . . . ' Of course I framed it and I use it in every interview—I put it in wherever I can. I have too much personality for selling carpets—and I was looking forward to it, too. It would have lifted me once and for all and separated me from all other composers, which is about all that I'm still interested in. It really is the one-upmanship game, isn't it?

As the Twig is Bent

It is very easy to get people to talk about their childhood experiences. For some reason, when the social conversation turns to childhood anecdotes we all have a few which we like to contribute. We may not be wholly objective or enjoy very reliable recall, but most people at some time scrutinise their early years for some clue to explain the adult they have become.

I approached this project as an interviewer, not as a researcher in child psychology. From the point of view of the researcher I have probably asked the wrong questions, for the discipline of the radio and television interviewer is not to gather data that can be easily codified and related, but to persuade his subject to tell stories which will, it is hoped, throw some new light on the human condition. The conclusions I draw, therefore, are not those of the professional psychological enquirer, but those of a fellow traveller through life, who may say: 'Right! That's exactly how I remember it.' Or, on the other hand: 'That's very interesting, but it wasn't that way for me.'

Personally, I had a very secure childhood—in fact, being an adopted child I would go so far as to say that I enjoyed a special sort of security. My parents never sought to hide from me the fact of my adoption and, in fact, I cannot recall a time when I did not know that I was adopted. In other words, I cannot even recall being told that I was adopted. It was simply a fact of life. My earliest memory is not of any particular event but of my mother describing to me how she and my father went to the babies' home and actually picked me out. I asked her to tell me that story over and

190

over again, with particular emphasis on the number of candidates. I wanted to know how many other babies I was superior to. That makes a child feel very wanted. I really wanted her to tell me of some vast number of babies from whom she chose, to confirm my belief that I was the most desirable of all babies. I had no lack of self-esteem.

My mother also used to say, when I misbehaved, that she would send me back where I came from. I have a feeling that child psychologists might not look favourably on that technique for ensuring good behaviour, but I think I always regarded it as perfectly fair. I was chosen because I was the best, but if I didn't measure up I could be sent back and presumably exchanged for a better one. I was sufficiently secure in my parents' love never to regard this as a serious possibility.

However, the consequence of all this loving security has been to produce a person who is no risk-taker.

If a child is given a secure, loving family environment with a great deal of encouragement and parental pride in its achievements it may tend to passively accept the moulding of its personality by others. However, in those cases where the child has experienced insecurity and anxiety, without the reassuring stability of a family bound together with strong mutual affection, the child itself becomes a more active agent. Note Anne Deveson's words: 'I was a very manipulative person, probably because of moving from one environment to another . . . '

All the people in this book can be divided up into two categories —what I would call the risk-taking creators (or as Kerry Packer puts it, the builders of Jumbos) and the equally brilliant but more passive people who have made their mark in a 'public service' type of occupation. In the former category of risk-takers I would include Bob Ansett, Anne Deveson, Pat Lovell, Fred Schepisi, George Dreyfus and Phillip Adams. These are the creators of new business corporations, the film makers, composers, free-lance journalists and advertising people. They exhibit an unshakeable confidence in their ability to survive in high-risk professions, or if they should fail it is 'not the end of the world'.

In the 'public service' category I would put Bob Hawke, Manning Clark and Gus Nossal. None of them has created the agency in which he works and all enjoy some sort of security of tenure. They do not appear as risk-takers. These three had very stable, secure family environments as children. Those in the risk-taking category had relatively insecure childhoods, variously experiencing broken marriages, boarding schools, forced migration and social hostility or poverty. They were thrown back on their own resources. The end result is summed up by Bob Ansett when he says: 'I had a personal disregard for my own safety. My only interest was in winning the game.'

It poses the question, is security addictive? Not many people would share Anne Deveson's confident enjoyment of travel in exotic places. 'It doesn't disturb me if I don't have anywhere to sleep at night. If I run out of money I always feel that I can find it again somewhere . . . It's not the end of the world.' That seems to express the confidence of a person who has lived through precarious times, survived them in fine style, and cannot be thrown into a frenzy by unexpected events.

It is conventional wisdom that children should be given a warm, secure, affectionate family environment in which to grow up—but would Phillip Adams have been the genius with words and pictures that he is if he hadn't had the solitary experience of his little sleepout? On the other hand what loving parent would subject their child to such pain to produce genius? Fred Schepisi seems to have come as close as any of those interviewed to having had the experience of being deliberately thrown in at the deep end of life by his parents and left to sink or swim. ' . . . my parents . . . believed they were doing the right thing and that it was toughening me up.' It was tough, but it seems to have worked.

The interesting odd-man-out in this selection of famous people is Kerry Packer. He was born to wealth and power, but even then only attained his present position in the corporation because his brother didn't want it. He doesn't see himself as a creator at all. To use his metaphor again, his father was the builder of Jumbos, he merely flies them. When asked about the creation of World Series Cricket as an example of building in which risk is involved he dismissed it as insignificant compared with the grand gambles of his father. Whereas Sir Frank had gambled his entire inheritance to found Consolidated Press, World Series Cricket represented no risk at all for the company. 'I could close it down and the place would not even hiccup.' It seems that the qualities of the gambler and the flamboyant entrepreneur who chances everything to create a new company are not innate but learned characteristics. John D. Rockefeller, Henry Ford and Frank Packer were all swashbuckling creators, their progeny, on the other hand, have all been managers of the corporation which already exists.

There is, of course, an obverse to this pattern of insecure childhood giving rise to the creative, risk-taking adult. For every Adams, Schepisi and Deveson who has turned adversity into victory there must be many more who have succumbed to neurosis and travel through life in a state of constant terror. Phillip Adams himself says that he is 'bloody glad that I had such a hideous childhood. Had I not had it I'm sure I would have just sunk back into oblivion in some way.' But he adds: 'when I first married I'm afraid I was so polluted by my stepfather's tyranny that I tended to react to it . . . I needed quite a bit of healing, which my young wife managed to provide, bless her heart.'

Nevertheless it is reasonable to ask, is there something addictive about security? The secure child passively soaks up the benign imprint of the loving parent and plays only a minimal active role in shaping his environment. Consequently as an adult he seeks the same sort of security and is fearful of being forced to survive on his own wits. Such people are common in the public service with its promise of 'permanence'. I would place myself in this category.

One question I have never been able to answer, as an adopted child, is which characteristics I have inherited and which I have learned. I know that I share certain mannerisms of speech and gesture with my adoptive parents, but I have no idea what I have in common with my biological parents. It is probably that mystery which compels some adoptees to seek their natural parents, but I must say I have never felt that compulsion. In fact I find the idea personally repellent because it would seem to me like a betrayal of the love I have received nearly all my life. I must stress that this is a personal reaction and is certainly not intended as a judgment on those who for reasons which must seem very good to them go looking for their other parents. But for me it is unthinkable.

As a child I had a natural aptitude for school work, with the exception of the alphabet which took me longer than the other children to memorise, and as we were only given our Second Reader when we had mastered the ABC I suffered some shame over this matter. I was also slower than most with the three-times tables, but that was not such a cause of embarrassment because the whole class recited these in unison and I could mumble my version of the table without fear of detection. I am at a loss to understand why these two exercises caused me so much trouble, because for most of my school life I did well at all subjects.

I went to Primary School in a little town in South Australia where three teachers managed seven grades between them. School was cheerfully accepted as a sorting process which would separate the manual labourers from the clerks, which was about as high as any of us expected to rise. It was accepted that a certain number of the students would reach the leaving age of fourteen before they had completed the seventh grade and they would immediately leave and go to work. There was no talk of slow-learners or remedial teaching. It was a brutal, efficient system, the justice of which was never questioned. As far as I can recall there was no stigma attached to those who failed to make the grade academically. It was accepted that some were born with 'brains' and others weren't. As Gus Nossal puts it more eloquently: '. . . that particular constellation of qualities that makes you a quick learner, able to comprehend things easily . . . to my way of thinking is indubitably genetic.'

One aspect of genetic determinism which was not generally accepted, however, was in the realm of sport. Like Phillip Adams, Gus Nossal and Fred Schepisi, I was an absolute failure at all sports. I simply lacked the co-ordination of hand and eye which is essential in even the barely competent sportsman. I was tortured and bullied by teachers who had an unshakeable belief in the essential 'teachability' of sporting talent. Now the very words 'compulsory sport' evoke feelings of shame and rage. I shall never eradicate from my mind the painful memories of my humiliating experiences in football, cricket, tennis and gymnastics. I feigned every disease I thought I could get away with. I suffered from ailments of the eye and ear as well as sundry gastric complaints all through my school life because it seemed to me that, with the onus of proof on the teachers, these offered the greatest scope for successful deception.

Related to my total inability at sport was my similar failure to learn the piano. To this day I am mystified by the spectacle of a pianist who can get two hands to co-operate to do two totally different things and yet produce an harmonious result. Charles Mackerras believes that musical talent is 'innate', and I wouldn't disagree with him. He says: 'Learning an instrument came very easily to me . . . and I was rather lazy.' There is a moral in that story for parents who believe that in their child there lurks a great talent which will be brought out by the discipline of daily practice. Where music is concerned, and Gus Nossal would say this of mathematics also, you've either got it or you haven't. All the practice in the world will probably result in only a small improvement in perfor-

195

mance, while the innately gifted will perform brilliantly with little or no practice. It is grossly unfair, but nothing in my own childhood experience leads me to think that it is not true.

Nevertheless, for all the importance of genetic factors in shaping the person, parents do contribute to the development of character. My parents belong to that category which I think is fairly common amongst those who came to maturity in the Depression—that is, mothers and fathers who worked *for* their children. Having experienced an economic catastrophe themselves they worked to ensure that their children would be protected from the effects of such a disaster in the future. It's a point of view which is not shared by, and indeed is scarcely understood by, their children. We were brought up in the years of plenty and assumed that our children would enjoy the same economic security that we knew in the fifties. Who knows, our children may have more in common with their grandparents than they have with their parents.

Reading the sixteen stories it is possible to theorise about the effects that parents have on the moulding of their children, but in some cases the conclusions to be drawn are too embarrassing to be written down here. But two cases stand out as being of special interest—Gus Nossal and George Dreyfus. Both of these men are the children of European parents. Both recall their fathers as stern and remote and their mothers as warm, affectionate and fondly permissive. Although both Nossal and Dreyfus are highly esteemed in their fields they are not in any way aloof, but are in fact very approachable, friendly and generous. From their own stories they are obviously more like their mothers than their fathers. They seem to have *inherited* their fathers' talents for scholarship and music, but they have *learned* the characteristics of their personalities from their mothers.

In most of the sixteen cases here it also seems that values have been learned from parents. Bob Ansett shares his father's commitment to free enterprise, as Kerry Packer also shares this characteristic with his father. Jim Killen learned his neatness from his mother. Bob Hawke learned his compassion from his father and mother.

The examples of Hawke and Killen also illustrate the extent to which parents can influence the political prejudices of their children. A few years ago I came across the information that most Australians have their political prejudices set by the time they are ten years of age. When I first heard that I leapt on it as some new gospel, so pleased was I to find that I was not a uniquely irrational political being.

I was ten years old at the time of the 1949 Federal Elections. My mother and father regarded Ben Chifley, as Thomas Keneally's parents did, as little short of a saint. To them Chifley was a selfless servant of the people who understood their needs because he was one of them—a humble engine driver. In R. G. Menzies, on the other hand, they saw a smooth, ruthless opportunist, totally foreign to their class and, indeed, hostile to it. I remember clearly my mother explaining to me that it was Menzies' policy to create a 'pool of unemployment' to keep the workers intimidated and docile. My father believed that if such a pool was created he would be in it. It didn't matter that he was a self-employed baker with a monopoly on the supply of bread in a little country town in South Australia and could only be unemployed if he sacked himself. They had experienced the Depression and they believed that Menzies and the people whose interests he represented had engineered it for their own benefit. Not surprisingly I lived in fear of a Menzies' victory throughout the campaign, and when it happened I lived in a state of breathlessness waiting for the axe to fall.

At school every Monday morning we performed the ceremony of saluting the flag. Only South Australians will believe this, so bizarre is it in its actual contempt for Australia, but this is what we used to chant at the flag. 'I am an Australian. I love my country, the British Empire. I salute her flag, the Union Jack. I honour her

King, King George the Sixth, and I promise Chifley to obey her laws.' At least that's what I thought we were chanting. After a few puzzling Mondays following the elections when we were still promising Chifley to obey the laws I raised the matter with my teacher, who I thought may not be aware of the outcome of the poll. It seemed that for four or five years of my time at school I had been promising 'Chifley' while everybody else had been promising 'cheerfully'.

My fear of Menzies naturally turned into hatred. Even as an adult, when I fully recognised the irrationality of it, I feared and loathed him. It is easy to understand the perplexity of Gus Nossal as a child torn between the popular adulation of Hitler and his parents' fear. I am sure that my parents wouldn't even recall discussing the 1949 election with me, because at the time it would have been a casual remark in conversation with a child—a thing of no consequence. The end result for me, however, is that it has never been possible for me to vote for any political party other than the Australian Labor Party. Rationally, I must admit to having met in the course of my work a number of Liberal Party politicians whom I consider wholly admirable and for whom I have the greatest respect, but I could never vote for them.

'Every boy and gal, born into the world alive, is either a little Liberal or a little Conservative' according to W. S. Gilbert, but the evidence suggests that political disposition is more a learned than an inherited characteristic. Compare Jim Killen and Bob Hawke, for instance. Hawke would no doubt agree with Killen's sentiment that 'The person who is physically, mentally or socially incapable of helping himself must be helped. I think the corporate strength of the community must be devoted to that.' The difference between Hawke and Killen is in the view each expresses of humanity. Hawke is an optimist, believing in the essential brotherhood of man. He is a socialist who is prepared to cast the welfare net very wide lest any deserving person not receive needed assistance. Killen, on the other hand, takes a pessimistic view of man, keeping a tight rein on the welfare purse lest any undeserving bludger should take advantage of it. It is not hard to see how they have learned their different attitudes from their parents.

For any person concerned about the future of the Christian Church there is a disturbing observation to be made from these stories. Phillip Adams, Bob Hawke and Manning Clark are all children of clergymen and Fred Schepisi and Thomas Keneally are both products of the Catholic education system and began training for the priesthood. All are now indifferent to religion or hostile to it. Schepisi's memorable essay into theology: 'If [God] exists I think he's a bit of a dill' should give the professional theologians, apologists and Christian educators pause for thought. The fact that all these men of outstanding intellect have rejected the Church to which they were so close in their childhood indicates that there is either something altogether spurious about institutionalised religion or there is something amiss with the way the Church represents Christianity to the world.

It is possible that the Church sows the seeds of its own destruction by solemnly advocating standards of brotherly behaviour which it cannot attain while acting with smug satisfaction and self-assurance as though it had already reached these lofty ideals. To Schepisi and Hawke, and perhaps to the others, this appears as hypocrisy, as though there were a deliberate intention to deceive the enquirer into believing that the Church is as good as it pretends to be and better than it is. The truth may be that the Church is a frail human institution which understandably fails to live up to the lofty ideals of the founder. The apologists might consider being a little more apologetic and less confident in their public pronouncements. Humility is a prime Christian virtue.

Keneally's comment that: 'If Hitler had gone to Confession he would have confessed to swearing at Eva Braun; he wouldn't have had any insight into his true sins' is a cutting assessment of the

Church's preoccupation with personal peccadillos and an almost total indifference to the grand, institutional crimes that make life a misery for millions. The silence of the German Church from 1933 to 1945 has all but destroyed the Church's credibility for people of Keneally's generation.

The attraction of the adolescent to religion frequently comes in the form of an attractive adult model. As Schepisi tells about his experience with the Brothers: 'I think they sense that they can work on you a bit and they sow the seed and you build on it yourself. Then one night you're sitting there with all the glory of benediction going on around you . . . and you think, Gee, this wouldn't be bad! . . . At twelve it's strictly the result of influence.'

When I was twelve I came under the spell of two deeply religious men, the first a young school teacher who boarded with us for eighteen months, and the other an itinerant children's evangelist who travelled around the country schools in South Australia in a caravan. He had a gypsy appeal that I found irresistible. Both were fundamentalists and believed that the return of the Lord and the Battle of Armageddon were imminent. There was also a remarkable old minister at our church with the same views on the coming Apocalypse. To a child these bizarre fantasies were more exciting than any fictional adventure story, because they were about to really happen. I positively revelled in it. Unlike Phillip Adams I asked no questions about the meaning of existence or my place in the scheme of things. It was really immaterial, because it would soon all be over. My one existential concern was that I not be found doing anything *dirty* at the moment of His return. This is not a facetious observation, but a real anxiety which I am sure grew out of that ignorance and uncertainty about sex to which Schepisi, Keneally and Nossal all allude.

Like Killen I was a precocious public speaker, discovering fairly early the power of the word. In the insular world of my little town there were only two classes of people who had contact with the 'outside' world, teachers and preachers. From an early age I longed to escape from the confines of the town and it was inevitable that I would look to one or the other as an ideal model. The preacher seemed by far the more powerful and glamorous person in the community. He was held in awe for his erudition and eloquence and he enjoyed considerable power in setting and maintaining moral guidelines. His presence in the pulpit was theatrical and confident. Only the preacher and the teacher among the people of our town spoke grammatically, being able to use 'did' and 'done' correctly without pausing.

All the subjects in this book were asked if there were any influential adults in their lives apart from their parents but none seems to have been influenced by as many adults as I was. Perhaps it was the realisation that my parents, who had given me much, finally could not give me an entrée into the world outside Williamstown that compelled me to turn to someone else for an exemplary adult on whom to model myself. It was virtually inevitable that I would become a parson. Like Keneally I don't want to 'run the priesthood [ministry] down, or myself, because I think the decision was made in good faith, but I think one of the attractions was this idea that you had power over your community . . .'

My children, however, don't attend church and show no inclination to do so. I worry that they are missing out on something that was very important to me as a child—but what is it? They say the services are boring and irrelevant and I can't argue with that. That is the public face of the Church. I tell them that what they see is not all that there is—that there is a body of people who, however imperfectly they behave, are the custodians of an important faith. But why should that impress them? If the timeless truths of Christianity are so valuable why are they not self-evident? Why do such truths need a special institution to preserve and propagate them?

In my childhood the Church was many things—a social focus of the town; a source of certain cultural values and information and a place that provided a satisfying ritual which met an adolescent need. It doesn't seem as necessary in a modern city. As a child I believed that Christianity was the one True Religion and that my particular denomination was the one True Church. That may have been astonishing presumption, but it certainly gave a congregation an irresistible *raison d'être*.

I don't share the view expressed by some of the people in these interviews that Christians by and large are hypocrites. Most practising Christians that I know take a very modest view of their own moral state. My experience of churchgoers is that they are very generous, kind, sensitive, decent people. If my life depended on the succour of any particular group I would feel most confident relying on the charity of Christians. Most voluntary aid both domestic and foreign which is generated in this country comes from Church people. Yet of all the people interviewed the Church has a significant place in the lives of only one or two. It is important to Nossal and to Killen, who regrets not being as 'punctilious' about attendance as he would like. For the rest it is either unimportant or positively distasteful. It's a point for Church leaders to ponder.

Parents are prone to blame themselves for any perceived defects in their children's accomplishments or behaviour. We shake our heads in bemusement and ask 'What did I do wrong?' There is always the fear that in our ignorant, uninformed handling of our children we are warping or scarring or in some way denying our children an advantage that it is in our power to bestow. Every salesman of encyclopedias and 'educational' books knows that this is the vulnerable chink in a parent's armour of buyer resistance. For parents who believe that books are the key to open up the world of knowledge and accomplishment for their children this sales pitch is irresistible.

Like almost everything else important in life the rearing of children appears to be a haphazard and mysterious process. Parents are as apt to be modified by their children as vice versa. Regard Gus Nossal growing out of his male chauvinism. Sometimes, as in the case of the Helpman and Mackerras children, there is a remarkable uniformity of talents and achievements. In other cases, such as that of Clifton Pugh and his brothers, the same genetic inheritance and environmental imprint produces three totally different men who have very little in common.

It is a strange and unpredictable process which produces unique individuals. In some future age, when human beings are no longer treated like objects, valued according to the scarcity of their talents, but are prized for their uniqueness and rewarded according to their needs, then perhaps we will be able to relax and enjoy this wonderful, mysterious process which cannot be organised and codified and made to obey our whim for tidiness.

Finally, the most valuable attributes for a parent are memory and imagination. The American author George Curtis summed up parental responsibility thus: 'It is a great pity that men and women forget that they have been children. Parents are apt to be foreigners to their sons and daughters.' Or, as Phillip Adams puts it, 'Childhood is a foreign country.' The challenge to mothers and fathers is to recall what it was like to live in that foreign country and to let their children know that they once visited it themselves and they know the way through—to persuade the child that it would not be imprudent to take the parental hand and be led patiently through to the distant land of adulthood.